CHIP CHOP CHERRY

A County Wicklow Childhood

RAY CRANLEY

Order this book online at www.trafford.com
or email orders@trafford.com

Most Trafford titles are also available at major online book retailers.

Print information available on the last page.

ISBN: 978-1-4120-1602-5 (sc)

Trafford rev. 01/13/2020

 www.trafford.com

North America & international
toll-free: 1 888 232 4444 (USA & Canada)
fax: 812 355 4082

Chip Chop Cherry growing wild
Along the meadow's grassy shelf,
What need has the wandering child
Of silver spoon or storied delph?

Chip Chop Cherry, luscious green
Food-store of the truant elf,
Dining out on fare as keen
And bitter sweet as life itself.

Cover painting by Peter Growney

For Phil, Rob, Lucy and Tim.

It was like this…

CHAPTER ONE

Ray parked his hoop under the kitchen window, carefully balanced his stick on top of it, and skipped in through the open back door feeling as sunny as the day itself. On his way he ducked his head under the hood of the pram that stood just outside the door and listened for a moment to the infinitely gentle breathing of his baby sister, Sheila. The warmth of the afternoon sun on the hood accentuated the clean sweet baby-smell from the pram as the little girl slept. He gave a small chuckle of delight.

As he entered the kitchen his heart was transformed from a butterfly to a ball of lead and went plummeting to the pit of his stomach at the scene before him. His younger brother, Val, was screaming blue murder as his mother stood over him holding his hands to her mouth, frenziedly gnawing at his fingers, almost hauling him off his feet as he tried to pull away.

'Now will yeh stop?' she glared at him through her De Valera specs. 'Now will yeh bite your nails again? Eh? Answer me. Answer me!'

Receiving only hysterical sobbing by way of reply, she launched into another assault on the tightly clenched knuckles.

Them flippin' tempers! Always spoilin' everything.

Ma was in full flight chastising one of her kids because, she claimed, their gobshite of a father wouldn't do it.

Ray hovered in the kitchen doorway holding his breath, wondering if he could slip out again unnoticed. He was sorry now he had come in at all, but having just

1

completed a record-breaking non-stop run with his hoop, all the way to the far end of Darby's Lane and back, he was just bursting to tell somebody.

The rattle and clang of the tyre-less bicycle wheel as he had puffed his way up the lane, deftly steering it in through the gateway by applying just the right amount of pressure to the shiny rim, had effectively drowned out the sounds of ructions from within the house, which would have forewarned him.

He took a tremulous step backwards. His heel touched the head of the sweeping brush that always stood in the back hallway and the wooden handle whacked sharply against the concrete floor.

Ma rounded on him, much, no doubt, to Val's relief.

'And you, yeh rotten get yeh, if yeh don't straighten up and get that hump off your back I'll kick the bloody guts outa yeh.'

Ma was the best mother in the world, she would declare, and couldn't understand why she had been landed with such a tribe of fatheads, all of them, it seemed, afflicted with some deficiency or other. Ray was doubly afflicted in that she maintained he had flat feet too, which she reckoned would surely right themselves if he would only straighten himself up.

She was famous for her tempers. Frequent and ferocious they were, and on the way home from school Val and Ray would argue in the lane over which of them would venture inside the gate first to see how the wind blew. If Ma was in top form, however, this little bit of reconnaissance was rendered unnecessary by reason of the fact that you could hear her halfway down the lane. On such occasions the two lads would prate loudly about anything that came into their heads in a doomed attempt at preventing their pals from hearing. The sting of the brown leather belt she larruped them with was more easily borne than the sting of mortification that left them cringing in the presence of their pals.

'Jakers, I'd hate to have to go in there!'

The likelihood that some dreadful worries lay behind these shocking outbursts was something that didn't trouble innocent young heads. They only wanted to know why she couldn't just roar and shout in her normal voice like everybody else when she got annoyed.

And she could be so heart-warmingly lovely at times.

It was a near impossibility to imagine Ma in a temper and Ma in good form as being one and the same. Her good days were like sunny little islands dotted here and there in a tormented ocean, and the children delighted in them.

They dreamed of how good it would be if it could be like this always, ever in the certain knowledge that within days if not hours she would once again be transformed into the holy terror of a Ma who never tired of impressing on them how useless they were and always would be.

And she told all the oul' ones.

Pushing the pram up Fairy Hill on a Saturday morning after shopping in Bray she would chat to whichever oul' one she happened to be walking home with, and the oul' one would be boasting about the latest achievement of her offspring.

'Now!' Ma would exclaim. 'Aren't your kids great. None of mine will ever be good for anything. Never!'

Dad was another kettle of fish altogether. Chalk and cheese had nothing on the difference between him and Ma. He worked as a four-pounds-ten a week gardener for the Sisters of Charity at Ravenswell Convent in Little Bray, starting at eight in the morning, cycling home for 'dinner' in the middle of the day, and finishing at six.

On winter evenings he would return to the convent after tea to stoke the furnace at the rear of the house, which provided heating for the nuns, and sometimes if the night was fine he would walk the couple of miles bringing Val and Ray along with him.

'Get your coats on lads, an' I'll bring yiz to the com-bent with me'

They needed no second bidding; nights at the 'com-bent' furnace were the best thing about winter - apart from Christmas, that is - and Dad was never in bad humour. On crisp starry evenings they would head off down the lane, and when Dad got into his stride on the main road they trotted along behind guided by the red glow of his pipe in the darkness, the sweet smell of Velvan Plug in the frosty air of the lonely Killarney Road.

Now and then he would take the pipe from his mouth to ask: 'Are yiz all right?' or to relate some anecdote about the Bray of his childhood, which had to be an incredibly long time ago.

When he opened the old furnace-house door a wave of warm air would rush out to welcome them as they entered the dark abode of this friendly fire-eating monster. A more intense blast of heat was released as he opened the fire door to shovel in the coke and they would gaze into the glowing mini-inferno wondering what the hell Hell must be like.

With the fire well banked down for the night a pleasant half hour or so would be spent soaking up the luxurious heat while Dad puffed away contentedly on his pipe. It was never that warm at home. They spoke in hushed tones and the furnace made its own fire and metal sounds. A place where you could happily stay forever in drowsy cosiness.

With great reluctance they would venture back out into the night.

'Goodnight, Mister Horse,' they would call to the stuffed pony in Foley the saddler's window as they made their way along Castle Street.

On up the quiet Main Street, passing the shops closed for the night, gaping wide-eyed in the lighted windows at all the things they would have when they got rich.

A funny word, rich. Ray didn't know what it meant, but any time he asked Ma when they would have some article of convenience lacking at home she would invariably answer: 'When we get rich.'

But where did you get it? Maybe it was something the postman brought, or something Dinny Byrne delivered along with the groceries from Caulfield's. Whatever it was and wherever it came from, he knew that people with carpets on their floors had it, and there were no carpets in any of the cottages that he knew of, so maybe it was just that the lane was near the bottom of the list for deliveries of rich.

He hoped it would come soon.

He had a feeling it would be good for Ma's temper.

At the top of the town the Divil would roar his stony reply to their half-scared goodnights, and Ray thought what a quare idea it was to put up a statue to the Divil.

And what did Holy God think?

Hands stuffed deep in pockets they would hurry towards Ballywaltrim and bed.

CHAPTER TWO

Dad had quite a collection of old records and the voices of people like Jimmy O'Dea, Harry Lauder, John McCormack, Bing Crosby and Gracie Fields rattled the windows of number fifteen Kilbride Cottages in the days before the family could afford a wireless.

They were played on a big old HMV cabinet gramophone that had belonged to Dad's parents and was given to him as a wedding present. Ray was a bit wary of the gramophone. It had scared the wits out of him one time when Dad was winding it up and the spring snapped sending the record spinning to the ceiling, smashing itself into smithereens. Everyone in the room - Ma, Dad, Ray and baby Val - had been showered with shards of record and sparks from Dad's pipe as he leapt back from the machine with a startled cry.

'Oh, be the lord Harry!'

This was shortly before they moved to Ballywaltrim. Ray was two years old and they were still living in the little front room of the old cottage at Windgates near Greystones, which had been in Ma's family since her grandfather's time. They had been allocated a new Wicklow County Council cottage in the late autumn of nineteen forty six, and moving house was undertaken by that time-honoured mode of conveyance, the donkey and cart, driven by Uncle Paddy.

It was piled high with bed, cot, Ray's wooden baby-chair, Nanan's Victorian clock, (her wedding present to Ma), the gramophone, some orange crates for chairs, an old table, several squawking hens and Toby the cat, and it was doubtless one extremely grateful donkey that reached the head of Windgates that day.

After darkness had fallen Dad had returned to Windgates for the rest of the family, and Val and Ray were pushed the three miles or more to Ballywaltrim in their ancient pram. Ray remembered looking out from the cosiness of the pram at the occasional glowing cottage window as they passed.

They made their way around the lonely Half Moon, the high stone walls and woods on either side intensifying the inky blackness of the night. Footsteps passed by heading in the opposite direction and Dad said 'Goodnight' at them.

'Goodnight to yiz. Grand night,' said the darkness.

'Who was that?' Ma whispered when the footfalls had receded out of earshot. She sounded a little frightened.

'God knows,' said Dad.

'An' what are yeh doin' talkin' to someone yeh don't even know? Are yeh a gom or what?'

'Ah sure there's no harm bein' friendly, is there?'

'God, I'll never teach that man!'

They walked on. Ray snuggled down and the rumble of the pram as it trundled along lulled him close to slumber.

'Won't be long now,' Dad said as they emerged from the narrow Boghall Road onto Killarney Road. A few hundred yards along they turned right, Dad pushing the pram up the stony lane. The lights of cottages showed on their left.

Ballywaltrim.

The last cottage at the top of the lane, which, unlike all the others, was detached, was to be their new home. They pushed the big wooden gate open and went in.

'Thanks bitta God!' Dad said as he unlocked the back door and flicked a switch.

A stark brightness made Ray blink and squint. A brightness from which there was no escape. That first experience of electric light after the flickering candles and paraffin lamp of Windgates was imprinted on his brain like an image on film. No cosy dim chimney corner with bocketty stool. No big tiles flagging the floor, just bare concrete. And no trellis room. Here all the walls went right up to the ceiling. Clean naked walls and empty echoes when you spoke.

A great black iron thing stood where the fireplace should have been.

A strange place. A cold place.

He suddenly wanted to be back home with Nanan and Auntie Kitty and Uncle Noel. Back in the warm safety of good old Windygap, as Kitty called it, where you could gaze into the big fireplace and imagine all sorts of wonderful things in the leaping flames. Where friendly fantastic shadows flickered on walls and ceiling and the black kettle sang on one hob while Toby purred contentedly on the other.

'Sure we won't know ourselves,' Dad declared, opening a door in the black thing. 'Isn't this a grand range? Look, oven an' all!'

There was a clanking sound behind Ray followed by a sudden awful rushing and gurgling that sent him running to his father's arms. Dad lifted him up, laughing.

'Don't be afraid, son, it's only the lavaterry.'

Ma appeared from the direction of the noise.

'It's a grand bit of luxury after Windgates, the indoor lav an' water.' She indicated the stoneware sink and wooden draining board. She called the sink a trough, pronouncing it 'throw'. 'No more trudgin' up from the pump with buckets.'

It was a scene Ray knew well; the women coming back from the pump at Windgates, heavy bucket in one hand, the opposite arm stretched out almost horizontally for balance, and a series of splashes along the path behind them as they went.

But now all of that was to become a dim memory. There was a whole new world to get used to and he wasn't even three yet.

Yes, and where would Toby sleep?

That winter was one of the worst in living memory and took a heavy toll among the older folk. The freeze-up lasted for many weeks and the snow was deep on the ground when word came at the end of January that Nanan had died. The boys were loaded into the pram and the family set off for Windgates in atrocious conditions, Dad going in front with the spade, digging a way through the snow for Ma and the pram. Four back-breaking hours later they arrived at the cottage where the lads were looked after by Angela Manweiler, the daughter of one of their old neighbours, while the adults attended the funeral in a blizzard.

When they got back the talk was of mourners slipping and falling as they followed the hearse down the steep hill to the new cemetery at Redford.

Spring finally arrived and Dad began getting the large garden in shape, planting hedges, vegetables, flowers and some fruit bushes. On a sunny day one of the orange crates was brought outside and the boys sat on either side of Ma to have their photo taken by Dad with his old box camera.

'Ah, for God's sake, will yeh look at oul' stormy fork there. Couldn't wait till after he'd had his picture took.'

A rapidly spreading dark stain had appeared on the front of Val's good shorts, probably the only wee-wee of nineteen forty-seven to be captured on film for posterity.

Their first wireless arrived around nineteen forty nine, rented for one shilling a week which was collected by a man in a little black Morris van with 'Brittain' on the sides.

'Bands galore there'll be on this. It'll be great divarsion!' Dad declared as he fixed it in place on the maroon-painted kitchen press with the wire-mesh doors, and ran a length of flex up to the double adaptor above the light bulb. The wireless was the first contraption to plug into that old adaptor and everything electrical that was acquired over the following fifteen years or so had to tap into the same source. The length of wiring that hung down from the ceiling must have been the toughest bit of flex in creation to withstand the treatment it was subjected to when Ma got her first electric iron, especially if she was in a bullin' temper. It was chucked, whipped and jerked in all directions, the crazily swinging light causing the kitchen to resemble a ship in a tempest. By some miraculous fluke the house was never burned to the ground.

The wireless soon took over as their main source of home entertainment and the gramophone stood mute in the corner, ousted by this wonderful yoke that never needed to be wound up, and never ran down slurring the singers' voices alarmingly as the gramophone was liable to do if insufficiently wound.

Much of Dad's record collection came to a violent end at the hands of the two boys. They devised a game whereby one of them would roll a record down the length of the kitchen while the other waited in ambush halfway along to roll a second disc at the first as it passed. On impact, those old 78s shattered in a manner most agreeable to uncivilised young divils.

They discovered their own favourite radio programmes. 'Dan Dare - Pilot of the Future' fought a never-ending series of battles against his arch-enemy, The Mekon, on Radio Luxembourg, and on Monday nights the BBC Light Programme broadcast a follyin' upper called 'Journey Into Space' in which even the voice of the announcer as he read the credits sent chills up their spines.

Ma and Dad listened to Irish Requests on Luxembourg, and on Sundays at lunchtime the whole family laughed at 'Living With Lynch' on Radio Eireann.

The big news stories of the day too were followed avidly. One event in particular that caught their imagination and turned out to be a real-life follyin' upper was the slow sinking of the freighter 'Flying Enterprise' in the English channel in the first days of nineteen fifty two. Ears were glued to the wireless to hear the crackling voice of Captain Carlsen who refused to leave the ship until the last minute, and each evening the photographs in the Herald showed her settling lower and lower in the water.

'God, isn't the sea terrible!' Ma would say. She had a dread of the sea ever since her Aunt Lizzie had ducked her under a few times when she had shown reluctance to venture into the water at the beach below Windgates.

On Grand National day Dad had a bob each way on a horse called Early Mist, and the family gathered round to listen to the big race. The pleased-as-Punch told-you-so grin on his face when Early Mist romped home the winner couldn't have been wider had he won the Sweep.

He invented the 'wheel' for them to push along in front when he brought them for walks along the country lanes around Ballywaltrim. A length of stiff wire was bent through the hub of an old pram wheel and the other end of the wire bent into a handle.

Sometimes after tea in the evening Ma would read the Herald for Dad. Like many of his generation he had been kept home to look after the younger members of his family at the expense of his education, and, as Ma put it, he was 'too bloody pigheaded and stubborn' to go and learn now. She would look out for any local deaths in the obituary columns.

'Aw God, Jimmy, do yeh know who's dead?'

'Who?'

'Poor oul' Jem Byrne.'

'I don't know any Jem Byrne.'

'Deed 'n' yeh do know him, a-course yeh do!'

'No'.

'Walked with a bit of a limp. Had a big nose - a remarkable snout altogether.'

'Can't place him at all.'

'Ah, for God's sake, a-course yeh can. He was always hangin' 'round the Divil.'

Much concentration and frowning from Dad, and scratching of his head with the stem of his pipe.

'No. It's no good. Doesn't ring e'er a bell at all.'

'Well, he's dead anyway, the Lord have mercy on him.'

'Aye,' from Dad, 'a harmless poor divil too.'

'What the hell do yeh mean, harmless poor divil, I thought yeh said yeh didn't know him.'

'Well, he's harmless now anyway!'

Dad chuckled and dodged aside as she swiped at him with the rolled-up Herald.

'Do yeh know what I'm goin' to tell yeh, Jimmy Cranley,' she laughed, 'you're the greatest oul' eejit on earth.'

And she went and stuffed the Herald behind the cistern-pipe in the lav.

CHAPTER THREE

Only Aunt Kitty and Uncle Noel now lived at the old home, in something that fell a fair bit short of harmony. Kitty was a regular visitor to Ballywaltrim. Noel only made the journey occasionally. Neither of them had married, 'fortunately for two lucky divils somewhere', Dad reckoned. Ma always referred to Kitty as 'the one in Windgates' and said she was 'as mad as a bloody hatter.' Nothing could guarantee a row as surely as a visit by 'The One', as the kids soon learned to call her. They would come running up the lane crying 'Here's The One! Here's The One!' Ma would say 'Oh Jesus!' and the stage was set. From then on it was just a matter of which of them would say the wrong thing first.

Kitty was never a fashion victim and she arrived one sweltering August day dressed in a big woolly overcoat tied at the waist with an old broken belt which had been put together again with the help of a couple of huge safety pins, while a third pin stood in for a buckle. Not to upset the balance of her outfit, her feet were ensconced in a pair of sturdy wellies, and the ensemble was topped off with a tight-fitting blue beret pulled onto her head. She stood in the kitchen doorway.

'Heh-heh. Good afternoon all. I've arrived! How are yeh, Lulu. Wait'll I tell yeh how lucky I was,' and she proceeded to tell Ma about the nice man who had given her a lift, and how she had explained who she was and that the man said he knew Ma.

'Oh my God,' Ma said, horrified, 'Yeh don't mean to tell me yeh got into somebody's car in that state.'

'Sure didn't he stop for me!'

'Even if he did, yeh didn't have to go an' tell him who yeh were for Christ sake, makin' a bloody show of me.'

'Heh-heh, I'm your sister, aren't I?' Kitty's voice was low and hesitant.

'Sister me arse. You're mad, that's what you are, do yeh know that?'

'Ah now Lulu...'

'Mad!' Ma interrupted. 'Who else, I ask yeh, but a feckin' lunatic would go out in the middle of summer in a get-up like that? Yeh should be locked up in Grangefuckin'gorman.'

'Well, this is a nice welcome, I must say.' Kitty sounded hurt.

'What the hell do yeh expect? God only knows who that man was,' Ma groaned. 'I can't hold me head up anywhere with yeh, comin' out here like Johnny Fortyfuckincoats an' the sun splittin' the trees.'

'He seemed like a nice man.'

'A-course he did. Jack the shaggin' Ripper would seem nice to you if he gave yeh a lift. Don't yeh know that all these people are only laughin' up their cuffs at yeh, an' you spoutin' all your business at them.'

'It's Noel, yeh see,' kitty explained. 'I'd be able to look after myself a bit better if I didn't have Noel.'

Ma let a shriek of mock laughter out of her.

'Jaysus, that's the best one I've ever heard. Talk about the pot callin' the kettle black-arse! If you were a proper sister Noel would be all right.'

16

'No, Lulu, I tell yeh he's the mad one.'

'Rubbish! Bloody balderdash! And then the state yiz have the house in out there. Lord God, I'd be ashamed of me life if anything happened to either of yiz an' a doctor had to be called in.'

Kitty's hackles began to show signs of rising.

'How I keep my home is my own business. If you had the likes of Noel to contend with...'

'Oh, laziness, have I ever offended thee?' Ma asked the ceiling. 'An' the cats. What do yeh want all them rotten cats for? Pissin' an' shitin' all over the place. Why don't yeh get ridda them?'

Kitty's face brightened a little.

'Ah, sure wait'll I tell yeh, Lulu, aren't there only six left now. Poor Frisky got killed by a car last week.'

'Oh Christ!'

'Yes,' Kitty continued, 'Noel was coming home from Belmont Wood with a brassna of sticks an' here didn't he find the poor thing on the road with her head all crushed an' guts everywhere, God bless us! He came home an' got the shovel to lift her off the road. We buried her in a biscuit tin in the front garden, a nice spot under the laurels'.

Ma stared at her incredulously.

'An' yeh try to tell me you're not stark starin' bonkers! Yeh think it's normal to be talkin' about curse-a-God cats as if they were Christians? I suppose the next thing is you'll be goin' to the bloody priest - God forgive me - to have a Mass said for the repose of the soul of the late departed pussy!'

Ma turned away to hide the fact that she was tickled by her own joke, and began clearing some delph from the table, muttering to herself:

'Sure she can't help it, the poor thing. The oul' mind's gone, God love her.'

Kitty had taken enough.

She whipped the old beret from her head and ran at Ma, lashing her about the head and shoulders with it. Ma, built like a whippet, scampered around the table, Kitty hot on her heels yelling: 'Yeh oul' bitch! Yeh bloody oul' rip!' and swiping away with the beret, sending kids scattering in all directions like startled squawking chickens.

Despite all their rows Ma and Kitty never fell out with each other to the point where they were not on speaking terms, and this was due in no small part to Dad's way with Kitty. She could be as cross as two sticks and he would have her laughing in minutes, and so by the time she was leaving that evening she and Ma were the best of friends again.

'Ho-ho bejapers! Will yeh look what the cat dragged in,' he greeted her as he arrived in from work.

'Hello Jamie, heh-heh.' Her pet name for him. 'An' how are yeh keeping?'

'None the better of seein' you anyway. Can't yeh see I'm on me last legs?'

'There now, I don't think you're quite ready for planting in St. Peter's yet'.

'Yis I am, an' won't it be ease to me feet an' them that are lookin' at me?'

'Heh-heh, you're a caution Jamie, so y'are.'

'Never mind your oul' slootherin' now, have yeh left me e'er a bit t'ate at all?' Dad enquired, mischief glinting in his eye.

'Ah now, I'm sure Lulu won't let you go hungry.'

'She mightn't have much choice if you've cleared the place out. Oh, an' I want a look in that bag of yours before yeh go too,' he waved a warning finger at her, 'in case yeh have tomorrow's dinner in it for the cats.'

Kitty went into a kink.

'Heh-heh-heh, ooh-heh-haa-haargh.'

'You're a quare eel, Kitty, but yeh can't cod me. I bet yeh have the press full of grub out there an' still yeh come over here atin' the bit outa my mouth'.

'Ha-haargh! Sure Noel eats two whole loaves every day. It's like feedin' a horse, God bless us!'

'Gerrawayouradat! Yeh probably have the poor divil half starved. Do yeh get up an' make his breakfast itself?'

'Of course I do. Doesn't he get a grand hard-boiled egg every morning. He doesn't know how lucky he is to have a sister like me.'

'An' tell us this, what time do yeh crawl outa bed at?'

'I suppose it's near enough to twelve usually, except for Tuesdays when I go to the Dispensary in Delgany, an' Sundays I go to Mass.'

'Twelve! Sure that's not mornin' at all. Yeh should have a good half day's work behind yeh be then.'

'Sure mark,' Kitty affected a 'quality' accent. 'I'm a lady of leisure, my good man. One lies in one's chamber until the call of the teapot galvanises one into action.'

'Yeh lazy oul'slag.'

'Heh-Heh-haargh!'

And so the banter went on until the time approached for Kitty to take her leave.

'If yeh don't mind, Lulu, I'll have just one more cuppa tea for the road, an' a cut or two of that nice turnover.'

Ma went to fill the kettle.

'Begod, aren't you the shy one, Kitty. Are yeh sure now yeh wouldn't like another dollop of cabbage an' spuds?'

'Ah, no thanks. I'd be afraid it might upset my tummy on the bus.'

Dad threw his eyes heavenward and shook his head.

'I give up,' he said.

When she had drained the teapot and left the turnover sadly diminished, Kitty burped like a stuttering tractor.

'Oh Lord! Pardon, heh-heh. Well, Jamie, are yeh goin to see me to the end of the lane?'

'I suppose I'll have to. I hope to God nobody sees us.'

'An' why might that be, may one ask. Are yeh ashamed to be seen in the company of your charming sister-in-law?'

'Yis I am.'

'Heh-heh-heh, y'oul shite. I daresay it would be a different story if I was dolled up like a film star.'

'Tripe is tripe, Kitty, no matter what kind of fancy bag it comes in.'

'Haa-haargh! Thanks very much. Well, goodnight Lulu, an' thanks for the tea an' all.'

'Goodnight. Mind yourself now in the dark when yeh get off the bus.'

'I will. God, it does be black out there. Sure Windygap is still the last car on the road, but it's home all the same. God bless.'

Ray accompanied them down the lane.

The Wicklow bus would take her to Bray where she would catch an eighty- four for Windgates. At the end of the lane they stood in the glow of the bottom light until the bus rumbled out of the darkness and came to a gravelly halt. As she climbed aboard she turned and called:

'Goodnight now, Jamie. Goodnight Raymond.'

'Oh goodnight,' Dad called back. 'Drop in again some year.'

'Heh-haargh-haaargh!' and she was gone.

They stood and watched the lights of the bus until it vanished round the bend as it climbed Fairy Hill, leaving the road black dark and empty. Ballywaltrim returned to the sleepy stillness the bus had broken. Far off on the unseen slopes of Little Sugarloaf a tiny square of lamplight from the window of Giltspur Lodge was all that relieved the blackness beyond the circle of radiance shed by the bottom light. Dad lingered awhile to relight his pipe. Even the scraping of the match seemed an intrusion. He smiled to himself and shook his head in the direction the bus had gone.

'Ah, God love her,' he murmured. 'Come on, son.' He started walking easily up the lane. It was a grand calm night, thanks bitta God.

CHAPTER FOUR

About three years after the original fifteen cottages were built at Ballywaltrim the council erected a small circle of ten further cottages in the field behind number fifteen, giving the lane the shape of a six or a nine depending on whether you viewed it from the top of Cattygollagher or Little Sugarloaf.

Up until then the lane had ended outside Ray's house at a big old wooden gate and from the various rungs of this gate children had watched with curiosity some men taking measurements in the field and hammering stakes into the ground.

When the foundations were dug out the site resembled an open rabbit warren as delighted kids scurried in the trenches with only the tops of their tufty heads visible above ground level. They took to calling the site 'The Buildings' and the name stuck. In Ballywaltrim you lived either up the Buildings or down the Lane. Officially they were Kilbride Cottages but most of the residents just called them Ballywaltrim, Ballywaltrim proper being a little further south.

Ma often recounted with a shudder the story of how one evening after a heavy fall of snow she had pulled on her wellies, climbed over the fence at the top of the garden and filled her message-bag with small pieces of waste wood to help keep the fire going.

Upon opening the door next morning she got what she termed 'an awful lemoner'. A man of grave demeanour stood at the fence studying the trail of deep footprints in the snow leading from the door to the Buildings and back again.

She was convinced it could mean nothing less than six months behind bars and for days was in terror of seeing a Guard's cap through the high pane of the front door every time there was a knock. Nothing came of it, but she swore she would never chance the like of that again. In fact Ma's honesty was quite remarkable and she would never contemplate trying to fool or 'best' anybody. If she found a ten-bob note on the road she would immediately have a note in the window of O'Regan's shop looking for the owner, even though she might not have a make herself.

From Ballywaltrim the view was of mountains on all sides except the east where through the trees a glimpse of the sea could be caught about two miles away.

On a summer's day Ray sat at the kitchen window gazing dreamily at Little Sugarloaf and wondering what, if anything, lay beyond it. A line of old pine trees stood out against the sky, bent into the wind like adventurers marching off across the shoulder of the mountain into the unknown beyond. Long before he knew of Enid Blyton's existence he called them the Faraway Trees. What wonders did they gaze upon from their lofty path? Or did they simply stare into nothingness over the edge of the world? Being enclosed by mountains left a whole other-world of fantastic possibilities open to his imagination, unlimited as yet by the confines of education.

He played with a sweet secretly-held desire to someday stand among those pines and see for himself what lay outside his own valley-world, but the idea that he might ever actually realize this ambition was incredible to his six-year-old mind.

He was stirred from his reverie by the sound of hoof-beats on the Lane, and as he watched, Johnston, Mooney and O'Brien's bread van pulled up to the gate. White-haired old Pat Shortt shouted 'Whoa!' and climbed down from his seat high above the horse.

Ray ran out the back door and over to the shed where Ma was tidying up. Dad had recently shifted the shed from the top of the garden because of the new houses and it was now only a few yards from the door.

'Mammy, the baker's here.'

'Right-o, I'll be there now.'

She emerged from the shed brushing the dust from her hands.

'Powerful day again, Missus,' said Pat.

'Yes, lovely, thank God. Have yeh any turnovers today?'

'Only one left, Missus.'

'I'll have that one so, an' yeh better give me a batch loaf as well.'

A big bread-basket hung on the back of the van and when Pat removed it and opened the doors an exquisite aroma wafted out making Ray's legs go weak as he feasted his eyes on the racks of lovely fresh bread. There were some cakes and currant buns on display too, mercilessly teasing his taste buds. Luxuries that seldom came any closer than smelling distance of Ma's purse.

'What are the pan-loaves like today? Are they nice an' crusty?'

'Of course they're nice an' crusty, same as they always are.' Pat put on a sham offended look.

'Oh yeah, sure mark,' said Ma.

He handed her a pan-loaf for inspection. After due feeling and poking she said she would take it.

'Right,' said Pat, writing into the account book, 'that's a turnover, a batch and a pan-loaf.'

'I suppose you'll be gettin' lots of extra customers now with the new houses,' Ma remarked.

'Indeed an' I'd be as well off without them. It'll only mean more work for me an' I gettin' too old for what I have already.'

'Divil a bit. Maybe they'll get yeh a motor van.'

'Go 'way! They'll never get me into one of them yokes,' he laughed. 'I'll see yeh Friday then, Missus.'

'Bye-bye, now. All the best.' Ma turned to go in the gate but stopped suddenly.

'Hey, wait a minute. Look at the bloomin' hole in this turnover. It's like a shaggin' grotto.'

Pat was opening the doors again.

'What'll I give yeh instead Missus. As true as God, I never noticed that hole now.'

'Murrya! As true as the candle ate the cat yeh mean. You're a quare hook, all that oul' palaver outa yeh an' you tryin' to stick me with a holla crust.'

'Sure what would I be tryin' to stick yeh for, an' you a good customer?'

26

'Ah now, go on. Yeh must think I'm a right oul' gom. Give us another batch instead of that thing.'

She thrust the offending turnover at him. He handed Ray a batch loaf and Ma went stalking up the path muttering about how you couldn't be up to anyone these days, that they'd cod yeh up to the two eyes if yeh let them.

Walking behind her, Ray picked at the loose flaps of warm fresh bread from where the loaf had been broken away from its neighbour, doing his utmost to consume as much as possible before they got back into the house. He was ravenous and it was still over two hours to teatime.

There'd be a quare temper if Ma ever got wind of it that Val and Noel Healy had pilfered a whole Christmas cake from the bread-van one day last winter while Pat had his back turned. They had jumped from the gap in the hedge and were back in Butler's field quicker than you could say 'Merry Christmas', breaking their prize into huge chunks with their bare hands.

Before he realized it he had made quite an impression on one side of the loaf, so when Ma left the rest of the bread on the kitchen table he turned the picked side so that it was hidden against the other loaf and went off out with himself.

He crossed the Lane and sat on the dusty bank opposite the gate. It was a lazy sort of day. Everything shimmered in the heat of the afternoon sun. Through the gap in the hedge he could see in the distance the new cross on Bray Head, and some barely discernible figures moving about its base. Dad said hundreds of people would be climbing the Head for the unveiling ceremony in September.

27

Behind him Butler's field was a sea of big white dog daisies where he and the gang had had great skit the day before playing hide and seek. The daisies grew so high it was possible to stay hidden for long periods of time because you could crawl all around the field undetected. He had found a pippy hiding place at the far end of the field near the quaint thatched Massey Cottage, and had lain there face down for over an hour studying the world of insects his nose was poking into, and breathing in the rich cool scent of the earth.

Eventually, when all the other kids had gone home, their calls fading away as they became browned off looking for him, he stood up. With his head just above the daisy tops he started wading through the long grass towards the gap, stopping now and then to savour the sunny silence that was broken only by the craking sound of the corncrake in the next field. He had never seen a corncrake but its ratchety call was as much a part of summertime in Ballywaltrim as dog daisies.

Sometimes on hot, clammy nights when sleep was slow in coming, the corncrake across the Lane would keep him company when all the other birds were silent.

The bread van came crunching and clattering back down the Lane, Pat yelling 'Cheerio!' as he passed. Ray held his breath until the dust settled, then, stretching himself out on the bank, he closed his eyes and let the luxurious waves of heat beat down on him. From somewhere down the Lane drifted the sound of young voices reciting an old question and answer rhyme.

'Where yeh goin', Bob?

Down the lane, Bob.

For what, Bob?

For Rhubob.

Can I go, Bob?

No, Bob.

Why, Bob?

'Cause you don't like rhubob.'

He felt good. The sun glowed red through his eyelids and the occasional bee had to be brushed away or some unseen insect flicked off his leg in case it might be a piss-the-mire, but all in all this was the life. If he felt hungry again he would go down the fields and gather some chip chop cherry, which was plentiful at the moment. That was the wonderful thing about summer; you didn't have to starve entirely between meals, not while there was an abundance of wild food of some form or another in season.

Chip chop cherry was a firm favourite with all the kids, its bitter-sweet leaves a marvellous thirst-quencher on sweltering days. Crab-apples, wild raspberries from Hodson's wood, bread 'n' cheese, wild cherries and berries and leaves of all hues and flavours were consumed in vast quantities as long as they were reasonably palatable, and there were occasions when this promiscuous dining out led to long unpleasant sittings on the lav.

In the garden Dad had some blackcurrant and gooseberry bushes and old Mister Valentine next door supplied juicy peas in neat rows whose pods hung within the greedy reach of thieving young arms stretched through the wire fence.

The chanting voices down the Lane broke into excited squeals as they were interrupted by a shout of: 'Any rags or bottles? Toys for rags!' from the Ragman, Johnny Moorhouse, coming slowly up the hill, his horse and dray gaily bedecked with balloons and other brightly coloured gewgaws to catch the eyes of the kids. They would all be running in now to pester their mammies for old clothes to bargain with, but Ray felt too lazy to bother.

'That's the boy!' The shout came from behind him, and he knew the greeting well.

Mister Lawless from number five was climbing through the gap. He worked as gardener for Butler's and crossed the field several times a day. Depending on who was in occupation of the bank as he passed, his greeting only varied in terms of number or gender.

'Them's the girls!' Them's the boys!' or for a mixed group 'Them's the childer!'

Ray said 'Hello Mister Lawless' and Mister Lawless said wasn't it well for him there sunnin' himself and 'That's the boy!' again and walked on down the Lane, his jacket thrown over his arm.

There were several gaps in the bramble hedge along the Lane, each named for the family whose cottage it was opposite, and they came into being chiefly because Butler's field was used as a short cut down to the main road into Bray.

Ray knew that once Mister Lawless had gone home it wouldn't be long before Dad appeared coming up the Lane, and that meant teatime. He got up, stretched lazily, crossed the Lane and climbed onto the top of the gate where he would have a good view as he waited for Dad. Then, from the open kitchen window he heard Ma's raised voice.

'Well, isn't that the right little fecker anyway. Half the blinkin' loaf gone an' he sleeveenin' along behind me, an' me only after makin' the other oul' twister exchange it for me. Where is he...Ray-MOND!'

She called him in her own peculiar manner; the first syllable on a low growling note, the second rising to the stars. It sent a chill through him. He leapt from the gate, scrambled through the gap and ran, bare legs swishing through the grass, until he came to Darley's pond. A startled heron lifted off from the water's edge as he approached. The locals called them cranes.

He looked around for some docks. In his haste he had run through a clump of nettles. He rubbed his leg vigorously.

'Docky leaf, docky leaf, take the sting of the nettle away.'

You couldn't eat docks, but the big leaves came in very handy if you couldn't make it home to the toilet.

The pond was very small, encircled by brambles, trees and bushes that in places leaned out over it, their reflections mirrored on its brownish surface. It was situated in the last field before the back road.

He sat on a strong bough and looked down into the water waiting for his heart to stop thumping. He could still hear Ma calling but at this distance only the '...MOND' was audible.

He would stay out as long as he could. It was a pity it was so close to teatime. Still, if he waited until Dad had been

31

home for a while she might have calmed down a bit, or better again, maybe he should stay out really late and let them think he was lost forever. They would be so delighted to see him that the picked loaf would be forgotten and the dreaded strap would be left hanging in its place on the back of the cross-door.

Countless tiny insects hummed and buzzed over the surface of the pond and all around him. He marvelled at their ability to avoid mid-air collisions. A water hen followed by three young chicks swam out of the reedy growth at the edge of the pond. He sat very still, delighted as the little family group came most of the way across to where he sat before the mother hen spotted him and did a quick turn, leading her chicks back under the protection of the overhanging brambles.

Mister Messitt from number eight passed across the field on his way home from his job at Martin's big house on the Herbert Road or the back road as they called it.

' 'Allo, 'allo, 'allo!' he shouted, his grey hair gleaming white in the sunshine, a half-filled sack of something or other thrown over his shoulder. Ray waved. He was beginning to feel sorry for himself now. Everyone was going home except him, and his tummy was grumbling. Jakers, he was hungry enough to lash into a plate of scabs. He began scouting around the field. It looked like chip chop cherry for tea.

CHAPTER FIVE

The boys found themselves back in Windgates for a three-week holiday when Ma had to go into hospital to buy them a new baby. Kitty was delighted with the arrangement. It was August and the world was at its friendliest. As with most folk of her generation, walking was second nature to Kitty and she saw to it that they were never bored.

In the mornings she let them take turns using the water-key with its handle shaped like an elongated teardrop, filling the chipped enamel basin from the barrel at the side of the house for their daily scrub. The smooth iron of the old key in the palm of his hand recalled to Ray's mind the woeful yuriary he had caused one day by sneaking it from its place beside the water bucket on the chair in the pantry and letting all the water run down the garden.

Their favourite walk was down the stony Ennis's Lane to the sea, passing an old tram that was used as a holiday home in a field beside the lane and talking to goats along the way, all the while Kitty entertaining them from her wonderful store of old rhymes and songs.

'Farmyard, farmyard, Come and see our farmyard.

Come and see the well with its water cool.

Sheep and cows and chickens in our farmyard,

Baa baa, moo moo, cock-a-doodle-doo!'

She would stop and chat with the folk who came out to lean on their gates when the laughter floated ahead on the summer air and told them someone was coming down the lane.

'Ain't them the grand childer, Kitty, God bless them! And how's Lulu, tell us?'

Then on across the railway track and down to where the surface of the lane had been scoured out into a deep gully by a small stream that flowed under the Gap Bridge and into the sea. The stream came from a well nearby that had once been the water source for the long-vanished Rathdown Castle. Trains had rattled over the Gap Bridge until 1916 when coastal erosion made it necessary to move the track inland for the second time. Great chunks of an older bridge still stood on the beach.

Ray's first ever close-up view of the sea had been framed in the arch of the Gap Bridge. He liked the way the waves made a peculiar echoing sound when you stood under it.

'Arches,' Kitty informed them, 'are designed by archytecks, heh-heh.'

She amazed them with her skill at making flat stones skip for long distances across the waves, and tried to show them how, chortling at their pathetic attempts.

Before setting off for a ramble she would leave the door key under a geranium pot on the windowsill and give the door a push with her elbow to check if it had shut properly, then after taking a few steps she would go back and try it again.

'Now! We're all set.'

Halfway up the path she would turn back yet again, muttering to herself, and give it another wallop.

'Be Christ, we'll never get outa here, heh-heh. Isn't it the divil altogether now, bad cess to it.'

Then, raising her voice to her bemused nephews waiting at the gate:

'Auntie Kitty will be with yiz in a tick, lads, never fear.'

One last hefty thump and she would stand back looking at the door for a few seconds.

'Right! This time! One, two, three!'

And she would fairly scoot up the path and onto the road, grabbing two small hands in hers as she went, hell bent on escaping from the demons that would drag her back to try the door again.

'Grand day, May!' she would shout to neighbour May Killeen a few cottages down, sitting outside her door knitting in the sun, while her toddler, Tony, ran up to the gate and chatted to them through the bars.

'Powerful, Kitty, thank God. Hello there, lads!'

'Ah, will yeh just look at the goin's of Tony, an' he hardly the height of a shillin' in coppers, God bless him!'

At a sharp bend a little way down from the house the centre of the road was marked by a line of white stones set into the surface, a forerunner of the painted white line, and on this curve stood Rose Cottage, an eighteenth century dwelling that was home to the Gray family. Roland and Norman Gray were big boys who took a devilish delight in Kitty's reaction when they rode their bikes towards her at an alarming rate, only turning aside when it seemed impossible that they could avoid running her down.

'Back! Back, I say! Keep...oh, yiz little shites, yiz, God pardon me. I'll tell your mother. Bess! Bess! Mind the children. Yiz have me demented, heh-heh-heh. Ooh, aren't they the scourges, now!'

For some unknown reason the roadside banks all the way from the head of Windgates down to Booth's Hollow near Blacklion had hundreds of seashells embedded in them, and they would collect them in brown paper bags. Even Kitty was at a loss to explain this phenomenon.

'But sure yeh wouldn't wonder at what yeh might see in Windygap.'

On Tuesdays they walked to the village of Delgany where Kitty attended the dispensary. Along with her tablets and medicine Dr. Finnegan dispensed a shiny shilling for ice cream from Brady's shop, three thick fourpenny wafers which they lashed into, licking their way along the winding road to Blacklion.

'Great tack!' said Kitty.

At Redford they called to Aunt Molly's.

'Molly'll make us a cuppa tea to help us up the hill.'

If Uncle Joe was home he would give Kitty some fish wrapped in newspaper, and he would tease her just like Dad.

'Fry them up for Noel an' yourself an' the lads.'

'I'm much obliged, Joe, the cats'll think it's Christmas.'

'Lads, if she gives them fish to the cats, you tell Uncle Joe an' I'll soon regulate her.'

'Heh-haargh! Go on, yeh oul' fecker, I only meant the heads.'

'Did yeh find that stockin' yet, Kitty?'

36

He seldom failed to enquire about the stocking stuffed with money which he reckoned Kitty's Aunt Lizzie had hidden somewhere in the cottage.

'I did, yes, an' a frog has feathers, too, heh-heh.'

Through Farrell's farmyard they went up the Slang to gather dead whins for starting the fire, and on a little outcrop they called Mr. Rock they would sit and watch the train, tiny in the distance, puffing its way along the serpentine track into Greystones, or follow the progress of a bus as it left the town and chugged up Jinks's Hill.

Set into the wall at the top of Windgates hill was a stone seat, built there long ago by their great-grandfather for foot-weary folk who, having trudged up the long hill from Redford, were grateful to rest their bones awhile before heading around the Half Moon to Bray. Kitty called it 'Tom The Horn's Rest' and would sit there and sing for them, her keen-edged warbling bringing the neighbours out to join in.

'There was a ship came from the North Country

And the name of the ship was the Golden Vanity...'

One sunny afternoon as she played chasing with them between the laurels, the sky suddenly darkened and huge hailstones hopped off the ground.

'Holy Mother, will yeh look at the size of them! Get inside, lads, run!'

In less than a minute day had been turned into night. Kitty felt around for matches and lit the lamp. She tried not to appear frightened, but her smiling lips were mouthing 'Sacred Heart of Jesus protect us!' unheard above the thundering of the hailstones on the roof. They came down the chimney, bounced off the hobs and went hopping clicketty click across the flagged floor like beads from some monstrous broken necklace. The fire hissed and spat as some of them fell into the flames. The din was terrifying, and Ray remembered Ma telling Dad how scared she had been in 1916 when the machine-gun on the roof of their lodge in the Phoenix Park opened fire. She was only six then. Was this what it was like?

From somewhere outside they heard a shout above the racket.

'Now who the flames would be out there in the like a' that?'

They all ran to the open door and peered out into the chaos. A figure, hunched over against the downpour and pushing a bike, scuttled down the path, and, throwing the bike against the laurels, made a dash for the door.

'Be the Lord Harry, that'd bate the brains outa yeh!'

'It's Daddy! Daddy!'

They grabbed at him and he hugged them.

'Ah, God love yiz. How are yiz gettin' on?

'Grand.'

'Well, I was never more glad to see anybody in me life, Jamie. Come in an' welcome! I was hopin' the lads wouldn't twig that I was a bit, yeh know, heh-heh, on the windy side. Is it the end of the world or what?'

'Divil an' end! But I never saw the likes of them hailstones before. Big as birds' eggs, they are. An' it the middle of August!'

'I'll make yeh a cuppa tea.'

38

She moved the kettle from the hob onto the fire and steam belched from the spout, but its song was lost in the madness.

'If you're hungry, Jamie, there's a few sausages in the pantry.'

'Grand, I'll have them with me steak an' onions.'

'Heh-haargh! Yeh will, yeah, sure mark. Unless maybe yeh have some in your pocket... Jesus wept!'

Kitty jumped as the sudden ear-splitting crack of a thunderbolt seemed to silence the hailstones for a few seconds before they resumed their hammering with renewed ferocity. Dad chuckled and calmed the boys, saying that Kitty was 'afraid of her shadda'.

'God bless us an' save us, I thought the bloomin' roof was comin' in,' she said, lifting the kettle from the fire and settling the frying pan in its place. Hailstones pinged into the pan.

'I suppose we'll have to make do with sausages an' hailstones, so,' he said, 'but first things first.'

He poked a piece of newspaper between the bars of the grate and lit his pipe with it. The weather could do what it liked now. Daddy was here.

As they sat to eat the din ceased as abruptly as it had begun, and the sudden stillness had an eeriness about it.

'Holy God Almighty!' Kitty murmured, and tucked into her bread and sausage.

'Goin' into an ill skin, missus,' Dad remarked.

'Snoink, heh-heh, snurk!'

Then, as if someone was raising a blind, the afternoon sunlight flooded into the room and you couldn't tell anymore that the wick of the lamp was alight. Kitty cupped her hand over the globe and extinguished the flame with an expert little 'piff' from between pursed lips.

'I wonder,' Dad asked when they had finished their meal, 'did any of them oul' hailstones get into me pockets. Have a goo there, lads.' He grinned and indicated his jacket on the captain's chair with the stem of his pipe.

They squealed as each drew forth a large cone-shaped lollipop from the Daddy-smelling pockets.

'Them'll keep yiz lickin' for a quare length.'

He wasn't joking; they were too big to fit into your mouth and too hard to take a bite out of.

'An' what about poor Kathleen, heh-heh?'

'Yiv a grand mouth, now, for suckin' lollipops, Kitty, but yeh may keep it for coolin' soup!'

Uncle Noel came in from his work on Darcy's farm.

'Hello there, Jimmy. How's everyone in Bray? All game ball, I hope.'

'Oh ay, all on the baker's list, thank God.'

Uncle Noel called the boys Valbo and Rayser. Wherever Dad moved in the kitchen Val followed closely, and he tended to do the same with Kitty when Dad wasn't there.

'A feckin' little folly-me-round,' Noel said.

The brothers slept in the little trellis room from where they could see the lights of ships far out at sea, and

40

hear the sound of the train whistle suddenly cut off as the engine entered the long tunnel beneath the lower fields. The room was separated from the kitchen by a wooden partition with an open trellis along the top, and after Val had fallen asleep Ray would lie and watch the dancing diamond-shaped shadows thrown on the ceiling by the flickering firelight in the kitchen, eventually dozing off himself, lulled by the low reassuring mutterings of Aunt Kitty as she brewed her bedtime cuppa. On exceptionally clear mornings they could see the far-off hills of Wales from the trellis room window.

When the time came for them to go back to Ballywaltrim Kitty brought them for a last walk down the lane to the sea. They could tell that she was sad that they were leaving.

'No more goats, no more trains

No more boats, no more lanes.'

She recited her own makey-uppy rhymes for them as they came back up the lane to Windygap and the welcome coolness of the flagged floor. When Ray was two those same flags had claimed his Puss-in-Boots mug as he attempted to pass it from his baby-chair to the adults at the table. It had been a present from Aunt Kitty. A lifetime later he would dig up the pieces while working in the garden.

'Her name is Rita,' Dad said when he called to bring them home, 'An' yer Mammy is dyin' to see yiz.'

A girl! A sister!

'Cheerio now!' Mrs. Mac's daughter, Teasie, shouted through the fuchsia hedge next door as they trooped up the path to the gate, Dad leading the way and Kitty galloping to bring up the rear having dealt with the door. Teasie was very

41

handy with the sewing needle and had cut down a second-hand adult garment to make Ray's first real coat.

The afternoon sun was hot and they were glad to get under the trees as they hurried up the hill.

'I'm wringin' with the parspiration,' Dad panted as they tramped over the head of Windgates and along by Lord Meath's Cottages. They stopped at the old Windgates Well near the cottages while he scooped up dripping handfuls of earth-cooled water for them. They drank their fill and splashed their flushed faces, then, refreshed, made their happy way around the Half Moon.

CHAPTER SIX

'Someone's yodellin' at the gate', Ma shouted to the boys through the closed door of their bedroom from whence sounds of demolition emanated. 'Why don't yiz go an' play outside on such a grand day an' not be stuck in the house annoyin' me?'

'It's prob'ly Noel Healy', Val said, making for the door. 'He said he'd give me a yodel if he was goin' up the wood.'

'Good Val,' said Noel, elbows leaning on the gate.

'Good Noel. Will we go up the wood?'

'No,' Noel sounded excited, 'Come on down to White's. The grain is in!'

'Aw lovely!'

'Lovelee!' echoed Ray, running down the path behind Val. 'Yeh can smell it from here.'

The unmistakable rich, pleasant, sourish whiff was carried across the back gardens and in through open windows and doors on the warm breeze. Soon all Ballywaltrim would know the grain was in. Every summer steaming truckloads of barley grain would arrive from Guinness's Brewery to be used mixed with various other foodstuffs as fodder for the pigs and cattle. It was unloaded into a concrete pit where it was willingly trampled down by the bare feet of as many kids as could squeeze into the pit.

The three lads ran up Healy's back garden and along the path through Darley's wood, which skirted the tops of the cottage plots. White's yard was already as busy as an anthill with trucks, pigs, men and kids all contributing to the merry din. The agreeable smell of the grain battled courageously with the customary pong of the pigs. The boys climbed out of the wood, leaving their sandals near the gap, and made for the grain pit where a number of children were stamping away happily, their shrieks of laughter making the place sound more like a funfair than a farmyard.

Cecil and Pat Messitt were there, probably the first to know the grain was in as they lived next door to White's. Little Margaret Power and Ita Healy, Con and Pat Carr, along with Ronnie Turner and the O'Leary brothers from up the Buildings.

The grain was very warm, hot almost, and Ray hopped from one foot to the other until his feet became acclimatized to it. Oh, the wickedly delicious way it oozed between his toes! He whooped and joined in the steamy war dance, the glorious vapours rising and filling his head.

'Will yeh just look at them kids,' farmhand Brickie Stalton said to George White. 'They're like horseflies on a cowshite!'

'Here comes another lurry!' somebody yelled, and several of the stampers jumped out of the pit to watch the latest load of grain being manoeuvred into unloading position. Shortly after it had come to a halt a scream of agony rose above the general din, and Ray saw the men running in the direction of the front of the truck. Now everyone was scrambling out of the pit to see what the commotion was about.

'It's Val!' cried one of the kids, 'It's Val Cranley. He's after hurtin' hisself.'

Ray ran to the lorry, fearful of what he might find.

Val had been standing on the bumper of the lorry when one of his legs had slipped down inside it. He had then lost his balance and fallen backwards. The men were now lifting him, gently freeing the trapped leg while he roared blue murder with the pain. When they let him down he fell to the ground, unable to put the foot under him, so Brickie and Gil White hoisted him up onto Mister McDonagh's back and he was carried piggyback through the wood and down Healy's garden. Ma was chatting with some of the neighbours at Healy's gate when Ray came running with his breath in his fist.

'Mammy, a man's carryin' Val home. He got hurt up at the grain.'

'Jesus mercy, Mary help! The bloody little get, I'll kill him. I warned him not to go near that rotten place. What happened? Where's he hurt?'

'It's all right Missus, it's all right. Don't be upsettin' yourself,' said Mister McDonagh, arriving with the casualty, 'He just gev the leg a bit of an' oul' twist. It'll be right as rain if he goes aisy on it for a while.'

Ma carried Val home and sat him on a chair where he stayed unwontedly aisy until Dad came in.

'Yeh poor divil yeh,' Dad said sympathetically. 'How did it happen at all?'

'Disobloodybedience, that's how,' Ma cut in. 'That wonderful thing called disobedience! Ooh, they love it. Love it, they do! Sure isn't disobedience a grand thing, eh? If that child had listened to his mother he wouldn't be sittin' there now with a broken leg.'

'Divil a break,' said Dad. 'Try standin' up there, son, an' see how it feels.'

Val gingerly eased himself off the chair, let a fairly convincing howl out of him and slipped to the floor, from which lowly bed he showed no sign of being in any hurry to arise.

The doctor was called and quickly confirmed that the limb was indeed broken, and that it was hospital for Val. Sheila was ejected from her pram and Dad pushed him to Bray in it, then carried him on a 45A bus to St. Michael's Hospital in Dun Laoghaire where Val nearly strangled him by swinging out of his tie as a nurse tried to separate them. He spent the following few weeks with his leg stuck up in the air encased in plaster of Paris.

'What's hospital like, Daddy?' Ray didn't think he would be too keen on it when Dad said there were lots of nurses there, because he had endured the off-putting experience of having a nurse call to the house every day for weeks to put a hot poultice on his head. That was the time he had stood up under the cast iron mantelpiece in the front room and nearly split his skull. An extremely large and painful abscess had resulted which eventually had to be lanced by Doctor Finnegan at Boghall Dispensary.

'Here's nursey!' Ma would announce each morning in a tone that suggested he should be delighted. 'Stand still for nursey now. Nursey won't hurt you.'

Nursey bloody-well did.

Just like Mother Anthony did at St. Patrick's soon after he began school there. He was delighted one rainy morning when Mr. Shortt from number five stopped to give him and Val a lift to school in the car he sometimes brought home from his job at Doyle's Garage in Bray. Alighting from the car at the Town Hall the door slammed on the middle finger of his left hand, leaving a big flap of flesh at the top of his finger opened up like the gramophone lid.

'This won't hurt,' Mother Anthony had assured him before lifting him several inches off the ground with a generous helping of iodine, and leaving him shocked at one of God's holy nuns telling a barefaced fib.

Val came home full of chat about lighthouses, piers and mail-boats, and singing a song called Moonlight Bay over and over. Shortly after he was discharged the mail-boat brought Uncle Jack and Aunt Chris for their annual holidays. Jack was Dad's only brother and the kids looked forward to these visits not least because it meant a staggering half crown each at the end of their stay.

On the Saturday before their arrival Dinny Byrne tethered his horse to the gate at the top of the lane and carried in an appreciably larger box of groceries than usual. Extra stuff like rashers, sausages, cheese and even a small tin of coffee for Jack who didn't drink tea at all. Most posh people drank coffee. Ray had never tasted it but thought the smell was yukky.

Still, if you had lashin's of money the taste of things probably didn't bother you all that much.

As she put the groceries away Ma moaned about how terrible it was, having to sink herself head, neck an' ears in debt to Caulfield's. That it would take her months to catch up, if she ever did. But it was the same every year. You had to do things like that when posh relatives came to stay. They couldn't be dished up a dollop of porridge for breakfast, a few spuds for dinner and bread an' scrape for tea.

No. The rashers would sizzle in the pan every morning for the duration of their stay, and a bit of meat would stew or roast for dinner even though it meant that these sumptuous aromas wouldn't bless the air at number fifteen again before Christmas.

Jack and Chris were rich. Anyone who went to live in England was rich. Rich and posh appeared to go hand in hand, and seemed somehow to affect peoples' speech as well. Ma tried to sound like the visitors when she spoke to them.

Maybe it was the coffee.

They more than likely had carpet on the floors of their house in England. Ray wondered if Ma would ever get her long yearned-for 'nice bitta carpet', or even the piece of lino for the kitchen floor that she talked about on her knees as she scrubbed the bare concrete which never seemed to stay clean for any length of time at all.

'Here they are!'

The visitors were at the gate. Ma and Dad rushed out the front door and down the path to greet them, and it was all kissy-kissy and huggy-huggy for a minute or so until Dad picked up the cases and they all trooped into the house saying so now and isn't that grand and well, well, well.

Ray, Val and Rita slunk shyly in the corner, in awe of the VIPs, while Sheila sat on the floor and waved Guggy, her teddy, at them. They kissed all the children in turn and the smell of posh would knock you down.

They had no children of their own, which struck Ray as being rather odd as babies must be very cheap if Ma could afford four of them and was talking about buying another. She had bought the first three at a hospital in Dublin, and the fourth one had been delivered right to the house in the middle of the night.

He had been awakened by strange voices and sounds that night, and in the morning heard Dad opening the door to Dinny Byrne, and Dinny saying 'Congratulations!' and Dad asking him in to see the new baby.

'Ah God, will yeh look at the size of it!' Dinny exclaimed. 'Sure yeh wouldn't see it behind a tram ticket.'

'Will yeh have a bottle a'stout, Dinny? A-course yeh will'.

Dad sounded all excited as he opened one of the four bottles Dinny had delivered with the groceries.

'I will begob, sure we'll have to wet the baby's head anyway, God bless her.'

When Dinny had left, showering praises and blessings on Ma, Dad, Baby and house as he went, Dad opened the boys' door and beamed in.

'Come on lads, an' see your new sister.'

And they had fallen over each other jumping out of bed, becoming all bashful as they entered the back room where Ma was looking all different and holding a little bundle of Sheila in her arms.

So, Ray asked himself, if Ma could afford not only a new baby, but four bottles of stout as well on the same day, how was it that people as rich as Jack and Chris didn't buy any babies?

Maybe they were much more expensive across the water.

Maybe that was it.

While the visitors were unpacking Ma darted around like a fart in a bottle making sure everything was spick and span. She chased the kids out into the garden, warning them not to put a nose around the door until the grown-ups had finished their meal. Her good linen tablecloth was taken out and spread neatly on the table. Crisp, clean and well ironed the day after Jack and Chris had departed last year, it had lain waiting for fifty weeks to be unfolded like the proverbial red carpet on their return. The tablecloths for the rest of the year were disposable ones with 'Evening Herald' across the top.

Before long the smell of food accompanied by the clink of cutlery drifted out to the banished children in the back garden. They jumped up and down outside the window, legs wobbly and mouths watering, trying to catch a glimpse of the delicious fare as it was lifted by the steaming forkful into the waiting jaws of the lucky adults.

It seemed an eternity before they were called in for their own dinner of spuds and Chef brown sauce. They accepted the fact that Ma simply could not afford enough of that fancy stuff to go around everybody, and anyway they were so famished it was hard to imagine anything tasting better than those floury potatoes.

And so for the remainder of the visit they were hooshed out to gawk in the window at the older folk stuffing their guts. Still, it was an exciting time for them and they loved it, and Ma usually managed to keep a rein on her temper when Jack and Chris were around, which meant a string of marvellously carefree days.

When the time arrived for goodbyes it was all kissy-kissy again, and half-crowns for the kids and something for Ma for having them. Then wavy-wavy at the gate until they were out of sight, leaving only a posh smell lingering in Ma and Dad's room.

The tablecloth was washed, ironed and put away, and Ma settled down to worrying about the bills.

CHAPTER SEVEN

As the days shortened the kids congregated in the early evening under the only two road-lights on the Lane, one just above Ray's house and the other at the end of the lane outside Power's of number six. On Sundays the men who played pitch and toss on the Lane all day would move under the top light as darkness fell.

The approach of winter brought extra chores, the most important of these being the gathering of sticks for fuel. Very few could afford to feed the hungry ranges on coal alone. One bag a week was as far as most folk could go, and this would be gone in a few days unless augmented by fuel from the woods. It wasn't unusual on a winter's afternoon to see an assortment of old prams and handcarts parked along by the wall where the road dips at Hollybrook waiting to be piled high with rotteners.

Ma and Mrs. Healy always went for sticks together, pushing their dilapidated old prams to Hodson's Wood where the youngsters played on the long natural 'slides' or in the Hilly Field behind the wood. It was a paradise for budding adventurers.

Running along the inside of the wall was a path at the top of a steep heavily wooded slope, and going down from this path was a series of slides created by kids skidding down between the trees to the banks of the Hollybrook stream. They were steep and bumpy and great skill was required in the art of ducking and weaving under the boughs of laurel which grew untamed among the larger trees in order to avoid decapitation as you came tearing down in a cloud of dust. Some of the slides ended so close to the tumbling waters of the brook that a lad needed to be fairly nifty on his feet if he didn't fancy an unscheduled bath. The girls and boys of Ballywaltrim spent many a happy hour on those slides, and many a ragged trousers saw the end of its useful life there.

The Hilly Field was a wide grassy slope with a level strip running across it near the bottom, about twenty feet from the river. This strip was a remnant of an old scenic drive around the grounds of Hollybrook House. Spanning the stream here was a sturdy plank that acted as a footbridge, with a wooden pole for a handrail.

At the far side, where the children never ventured, a crooked path disappeared upward into dense woodland. The place had a charming fairy tale quality about it, and, adding to this air of mystery, a little girl would sometimes appear out of the woods and cross the footbridge to play with the children, and their cries of delight as they rolled and tumbled in the Hilly Field would gladden the air of that special place until the mothers called from the wood that it was time to go home. Then little Mary - her name was all they knew about her - would vanish into the trees on the opposite side again. They thought it must be exciting to live in the woods, but maybe a bit creepy at night.

Val and Ray would run back through the wood with the other kids and throw the sticks Ma had gathered over the wall while she loaded them into the pram outside. Then the little wagon train would wend its way back to the cottages.

Later, when they were considered big and ugly enough to go off for firewood themselves, the two lads and some of their cronies were allowed go to the wood without parental supervision, and from then on Hodson's, or 'Hudson's' as they called it, became the most frequented wood in the area, and was utilized to its fullest potential as a playground.

The after-school fuel gathering forays were eagerly anticipated. They would head off for hours on end followed by Ma's wasted admonition not to 'tear the arse out of your trousers on them oul' slides.' They carved their initials and those of their 'girlfriends' in the trunks of the great beeches. Ropes were carried to tie up the brassnas of sticks and there was friendly rivalry over who gathered the biggest brassna. Then as they staggered homeward laden like beasts of burden the cry would go up from some waster leaning on a gate:

'Hey, where are yiz goin' with the fuckin' birds' nests?'

Keeping the home fires burning during long wet spells was no picnic. One rainy Saturday afternoon just before Christmas Ray accompanied Dad to the wood. There was seldom enough fuel to have fires in the small bedroom grates and the idea was to get some extra sticks in so they might at least enjoy the comfort of having them lit over the festive season.

'Sticks', he said, 'is the best value firin' yeh can get. They'll warm yeh up three times over. Gatherin' them, cuttin' them up, an' burnin' them.'

He said it would be too slippery in the part of the wood where the slides were, so instead they turned up Hodson's lane beside the wood and after a short walk climbed into a field and crossed it to a different strip of woodland which separated two fields, where he laid his rope out straight on the ground and began searching for decent bits of wood to lay across it.

Tree trunks shone with rain running down them in sheets, and father and son were wet, cold and miserable, but Dad gave him one of his own funny winks and everything was all right. The pair of old socks Ray had pulled onto his hands as gloves were thoroughly soaked and worse than useless so he stuffed them into his pocket and held his hands under his oxters for warmth.

When Dad had gathered as much as he could carry he pressed one foot on the bundle and pulled the rope tight, then blew on his numb fingers.

'It's turnin' to sleet, tonight'll be a real geranium killer. God, I'm gummin' for a smoke.'

Rainwater dripping from the drenched trees extinguished about half a dozen matches before he managed to get his pipe going. He took long deep pulls.

'Ah, that's puff puff got it puff at last! puff puff puff.

The smell of tobacco smoke permeated the wet misery of the December afternoon, to Ray the smell of comfort and safety. Dad threw his brassna across his shoulders.

'Let's get home outa this in the name a' God.'

Ray grabbed a bough that lay nearby and dragged it behind him. Every little helped.

Darkness was falling as they climbed out onto Giltspur Lane - that was its proper name - gloomy now under its woody cloak, and he was glad he wasn't alone. On their way down to the main road they passed a tiny whitewashed cottage at a sharp bend in the lane, its small windows glowing cosily. He didn't know it then but this was the home of the mysterious little Mary Ryan who came to play with the children in the Hilly Field on days so very much different to today.

His bough kept catching in things and jerking out of his frozen hands but he was determined to get it home. On the main road they passed Andy Fitzsimon's little shop and inside Andy was serving Dan Buckley with a paper packet of five Woodbines. Andy waved out to them and Dan called in his strong Cork accent:

'How are 'oo, Mister Cranley? Shocking evening. Happy Christmas to ye!'

Dad plucked the dudeen from his mouth.

'Same to you, an' many of them!'

Sometimes two local girls, Maura Power from number six and Tiny McCabe of Kilcroney Lane helped out as assistants at Andy's.

The light thrown from the shop window caught the raindrops dancing in the puddles.

It was the only light to be seen on that stretch of road as they squelched on. Lawlor's lodge at the gates of Westmoreland, the haunted house, was in darkness, but the bottom light in the Lane gleamed ahead of them through the sleety rain, guiding them home, and they were thankful that no car came along to throw showers of freezing water over them.

'Daddy.'

'Yis, son?'

'Why does Mammy say she hates Christmas?'

56

'Ah, she doesn't really hate it. It's just that she does be terrible worried about not havin' enough money for the few extra things we do need to get in.'

'Will there be enough money for Santy?'

'Ah, God love yeh, a-course there will. Don't worry son, Daddy Christmas'll come no matter what.'

They deposited their sticks in the shed, and having kicked the mud off their feet went in the back door. Ma, on her knees in front of the range, turned as they entered.

'D'yeh know what it is? They should be shot, the whole bloody lot of them.'

'Who should? Why?' asked Dad.

'Them shaggers of coal merchants, that's who. I ordered two bags a' turf insteada one bag a' coal this week, thinkin' it would stretch a bit further, an' will yeh just look at the muck they sent.'

Dad picked a sodden lump from the bucket.

'It'd take a quare spark to get that goin' all right. Is it all like that?'

'Every last lousy bit of it. Now how in the name a' Jaysus Christ crucified do they expect poor people to burn the like a' that?'

'I'll tell yeh what,' Dad offered, 'I'll chop up a few of the sticks we got an' maybe we'll be able to dry the sods out on top of the range.'

'Indeed it'd answer yeh better to go down to Bray an' eat the shite outa them for sendin' such muck.'

She continued unloading the soggy mess of burnt newspapers and turf from the range.

'This is the third time I've had to take the whole shaggin' lot back out, an' I'm sick an' tired of it. The fire should be lightin' long ago, so yiz can sing for your feckin' supper tonight.'

'Ah, don't start now, it's Christmas. The poor kids...'

'Yes,' she interrupted, 'it's Christmas. More money. More bloody debt. I'm supposed to do Merry Merlin with a few lousy shillin's that wouldn't pay half what we owe, let alone buy extra for Christmas. I dread the bloody thoughts of it, so I do.'

She tore some newspaper to shreds.

'Don't try it again yet,' Dad said, heading for the door. 'I'll go an' get the sticks in now.'

Ray took off his wet things, dried himself with a towel and got into his pyjamas. The house was cold. He had looked forward to coming home to a blazing fire.

Dad came back with an armful of kindlers, loaded them into the range on top of the paper and put a match to it. The sticks, being none too dry themselves, were taking their time about catching, so he took a full page of newspaper and held it against the front of the grating, making the flames roar up the chimney with alarming ferocity.

'That'll do the trick,' he grinned, clenching his pipe between his teeth.

'Ay,' said Ma, 'won't it be a grand trick now if yeh set the blinkin' chimney on fire.'

'Divil a fear.'

He took the paper away and the fire crackled on merrily. Outside the wind was rising and sleet lashed against the windows.

The range warmed up and Ma calmed down.

'Janey, will yeh listen to that. It sounds like a terrible night out there,' she said.

'Yis,' Dad replied, 'wouldn't yeh nearly bring in the gate.'

CHAPTER EIGHT

He danced from one foot to the other with excitement and anticipation as he stood with Ma and Val in the rain at Billy Wilde's shop on the corner of Florence Road. They were waiting for Aunt Kitty who had promised to bring Ray and his cousin, Marie Quinn, to Dublin on the train as a Christmas treat.

He was very fond of Marie. They always had great skit together when she came to visit Ballywaltrim with Aunt Molly and Uncle Joe in their pony and trap.

Across the street the church steps had become a series of miniature waterfalls forming wide streams that flowed from the gates to join the waters that were rushing down the gutters of the Main Street and gurgling into the drains.

Val bawled his head off when he realized he wasn't included in the planned trip, and Ma had to haul him back up the street while Kitty steered her two eager charges towards the railway station. She pushed them ahead of her into the carriage.

'All aboard the Puffing Billy! Steady now, steady, heh-heh.'

Ray had never been on a train before, nor had he ever set foot in Dublin. The great shops dazzled and mesmerised him, most of them so much bigger than anything in Bray. An unbelievable array of marvels on display before his delighted eyes.

In Woolworth's Kitty bought him a little toy car and if the grip he held on it was anything to go by it might have been made of solid gold. At dusk the Christmas lights came

60

on, transforming the city into a wonderland of colour, reflected like some magical underwater world in the rain-shining streets.

Dealers shouted their wares in warm singsong Dublin accents from behind stalls laden with toys, decorations, gaudy jewellery and an abundance of good things to eat. He was nearly overcome by the strange magic of it all.

Coming upon a group of carol singers braving the elements under a large umbrella, Kitty joined in their rendering of 'The First Noel', her voice rising clear above those of the singers and the din of the city. She finished the song one word behind the group, delivering the final 'I-I-Is-ra-el!' with great gusto, and allowing it to peter out into a soft 'heh-heh.'

At Mass on Sundays she employed the same device, finishing each prayer a little behind the rest of the congregation, her sonorous 'Amens' reverberating round the church for all to admire.

She frequently informed her friends that her schoolteacher had been of the opinion that she could go far with her sweet voice, and goodness only knew to what heights she might have soared had she not been shipped off to Windgates against her will and before her schooling was completed, to live with her spinster Aunt Lizzie in what she called that unlucky year of nineteen twenty six.

Never one to 'blush unseen', she would burst into song at the slightest encouragement from almost anyone, whether acquaintance or total stranger.

They waited, panned out but happy, in the huge Westland Row station until the great steam-belching engine

61

came chuffing and hissing out of the darkness to carry them back to Bray.

Before teatime on Christmas Eve Dad lit the big red candle and drew back the curtains a little so the glow might be seen from the lane. The same little ritual was probably being performed in all of the cottages. It would shine again in the window when they stood on the front step to hear the bells of Christ Church ring in the new year, and finally on Old Christmas Eve, before being stored away with the four paper garlands that radiated from the light to the corners of the room.

Tea over, Ma washed them all and, impatient for morning, they climbed into bed. After all her threats to the contrary she assured them that Santy would indeed be coming to number fifteen.

Ray couldn't sleep. He lay for hours listening to the busy sounds of preparation from the kitchen. The smell of singed feathers drifted in as Ma held a lighted newspaper under the chicken she had plucked to burn off the remaining stubble. At one point Dad gently opened the bedroom door and stuck his head in. He stopped his humming of Adeste Fideles and listened for a few seconds, then withdrew to the kitchen.

'I think they're dead to the world, the poor divils,' he whispered.

There followed much rustling of paper and muttering in low tones. He could hardly resist the temptation to peep. From the wireless, turned down very low, came the comforting sound of Christmas carols.

At last all noises ceased and he heard his parents going to bed. The smell of the big paraffin lamp mingled with the other seasonal scents. Ma lit it to avoid having to get out of bed to switch the electric light off.

Their voices came to him in indistinct mumblings for a while, then all was silent except for the familiar tick-tock of Nanan's old clock.

He pulled the covers right up over his cold nose. The heavy old coats thrown over the bed for extra warmth tickled him and his nose twitched rabbit-like. Footsteps sounded out on the Lane, crunching in the stillness and fading away towards the Buildings. Who could it be, out so late on Christmas Eve? He hoped Santy wouldn't see whoever it was and decide not to stop at the lane at all.

Maybe it was Santy!

The last thing he heard as he drowsed into a contented sleep was the far-away lonesome sound of a train whistle at Bray station.

He awoke to the crashing, clanging and scraping of Ma cleaning out the range. It was still dark and freezing cold. Keeping the covers up around him he poked his foot towards the end of the bed. Jakers, it was like ice down there, but yes, he was rewarded by the feel of something heavy on the bed. He lifted his head and in the small amount of light that filtered in from the kitchen he could make out the brown paper parcel.

He made a mad dive and tore excitedly at the neat wrapping.

'Val, Val! Santy came. Wake up!'

Without a word and with his eyes still closed Val jumped up and was ripping the paper from his own parcel.

'Snakes an' Ladders!' Ray held up the gaily-coloured box.

'I got Ludo,' said Val, 'an' a torch.'

'I got one too. Hey, now we can read comics under the bedclothes. Pippy!'

Exclamations of delight greeted each item as it was drawn out.

'A box of paints an' a paintin' book!

'Ooh, a packet of Rolo!'

'An Orange!'

And wasn't it amazing how Santy knew that their favourite apples were the huge yellow ones Dad brought home from the convent garden. They spread their treasures on the beds and feasted their eyes on them for a while before making a dash for the kitchen.

'Mammy, Santy came! Look what we got!'

'Well, glory be to Christmas, the day we get the beef!'

It was an expression Ma used often and at any time of year, and it must have been an old Dublin saying because she always sounded like one of the stallholders when she said it. Its significance eluded Ray because today was Christmas and there was no sign of any beef, any more than there had been at any other of the few Christmases he could remember, only the red hen that Ma had chopped the head off when Dad refused to wring its neck.

64

The unfortunate decapitated fowl had scuttled crazily around the back garden, kids jumping terrified out of its way as it sprayed blood in all directions, Ma chasing after it with the bloodstained hatchet still clutched in her hand, while its surprised looking head lay on the doorstep.

Now! Isn't Santy a grand man,' she said, looking appropriately astounded as the presents were held up for her appreciation. The boys were shivering.

'Go on back to bed till I have the fire lightin', an' then I'll get yiz ready for Mass. I don't want yiz wakenin' the girls yet.'

Ma had already been to Mass and would get the dinner and Christmas pudding on as soon as Dad and the boys were on their way. Dad looked as neat as ninepence in his navy pinstripe suit. He rubbed some come-back into his hair, put on his good soft hat at just the right angle, and he was ready for royalty.

'Such titivatin'!' Ma, scoffed. 'Who the hell do yeh think you're goin' to meet?'

'Ah now, yeh never know. Some grand mot might take a fancy to me.'

He winked at the boys who were standing shiny-faced and ready, a copy of 'The Little Ones' Prayer Book' in their fists.

'Deed 'n' who'd look at yeh? God help your wit.'

'Yid be surprised now,' he grinned, 'an' anyway won't The One be comin' later. I have to be lookin' me best for her, don't I?'

'Feck off an' don't make me curse on Christmas mornin', y'oul eejit.'

On the road to Bray they met many people returning home from earlier Masses and 'Happy Christmas's' were flying around like snowflakes.

Dad lifted his hat to all the ladies including Daisy Dunne, the local femme fatale, who as usual looked as smart as a newly scraped carrot, perfectly made up and sporting the latest hairstyle. Dad remarked that she was Greta Garbo spat out.

'Good morning, Mister Cranley. Happy Christmas!'

The words dripped from Daisy's bright red lips as she glided by, hips rolling and not a hair out of place.

After Mass they knelt for a while at the big crib inside the church door. Ray found it hard to reconcile the cosy scene before him with the cold stable described in the Christmas story, and only the animals' breaths to warm the baby Jesus. In fact he could almost envy the child lying there in his bed of straw, bathed in the soft light of a star that shone through a small red-paned window at the back of the stable.

The kitchen was as warm as toast when they got back home, the pudding bubbling away in the big iron pot on the range and Ma busy preparing vegetables. Kitty arrived around midday, more suitably attired on this occasion in the same rig-out she had worn in August.

'Merry Christmas all, and many happy returns, heh-heh. I've arrived!'

'Oh, never fear, the bad penny will always turn up', said Dad. 'Where's me present?'

'Heh-heh-heh, isn't my company present enough for yeh?'

'Kitty, d'yeh know what it is, your company would be more than enough for anyone. No present! Well, yeh miserable oul' bitch.'

'Oh, God bless us and save us!' Kitty feigned shock. 'Isn't that a nice way to speak to a body in the season of goodwill. I'm surprised at yeh, Jamie.'

'Ah, take off your coat an' sit down outa that.'

'Heh-heh, thanks, I will.'

She took some bars of chocolate from her old message-bag of multi-coloured leather patches and handed them to the kids. Ma raised a warning finger.

'No muck before dinner now.'

Whatever other little deficiencies Kitty may have been afflicted with, there was certainly nothing the matter with her appetite. At dinner she put away an amazing amount. Dad asked her if she had seen White's horse on the lane as she had come up. She said she hadn't and Dad said it was a good job because she would probably have 'et the bloody thing for starters.'

'Heh-gulp-ha-haargh-haaargh,' she spluttered bits of food across table.

'Oooh, Jamie, don't make me laugh for God's sake. I'll burst!'

'Begod I won't, so.'

When the hot Christmas pudding smothered in custard was served Ray ate it as slowly as he could, making it

67

last. He did the same with his jelly every Sunday. Reluctant to eat the last spoonful, he would not allow himself to do so until he had fixed his mind on some future treat that lay in store for him, like spending a threepenny bit in Andy's on a 'load of bloody stickjaw.'

Dad wound up the gramophone and they laughed along with Harry Lauder as he sang 'Stop Your Ticklin' Jock' and 'It's Nicer to lie in Bed.' John McCormack and Bing Crosby took turns crooning 'Silent Night' and Jimmy O'Dea had them all singing the chorus of 'The Charlady's Ball'.

Dad said wasn't it great divarsion and Ma said wouldn't Jimmy O'Dea make a cat laugh, which prompted Kitty to start relating the latest adventures of the cats in Windgates, which in turn sparked off the customary row between her and Ma.

They railed away at each other for an hour or so, Kitty blaming all belonging to her, dead and alive, for her present unfortunate position in life, and Ma telling her in tones that would shame a cut-throat razor that the cure for all her ills was to get up off her lazy arse and do a bit of work.

'Will yiz shut up outa that for the luvva God,' an exasperated Dad finally interrupted. 'Can yiz not act like Christians even on Christmas Day?'

The row climaxed when Ma promised Kitty that she would pray for her to Saint Luke, adding that he had a great reputation for helping the hopeless. Kitty shrieked and stamped her left foot.

'How dare you speak to me like that, you rotten bitch. I am your senior and you have no right to tell me how to live my life.'

She was a year older than Ma.

'How dare you, I say!'

Then suddenly as if someone had pulled a plug she very quietly said:

'Anyway, Jamie's right. We shouldn't be fightin' today.'

'I suppose we shouldn't,' Ma agreed in a similarly sudden transmogrification.

And that was it. They sat back, sated, and swapped the latest gossip.

'That's more like it,' Dad said. 'I declare to God yiz are as contrary as the two ends of an S-hook.'

After tea Kitty played board games with the lads, moving the counters with the permanently crooked little finger of her left hand, much to the amusement of her wicked nephews whose ill-concealed giggles she probably put down to their enjoyment of the game.

And she sang for them in her inimitable style songs that they would forever associate with her: 'D'ye Ken John Peel', 'No, John, No' and their favourite, a ballad about a ship called 'The Golden Vanity'.

Ma cut a generous chunk out of the Christmas cake and another from the pudding for Kitty to bring home to Noel.

'He'll be charmed with that, Lulu,' she said as she stuffed it into her bag.

'Ay, if he ever sees it,' said Dad.

'Ah now, Jamie, yeh don't think I'd eat it all myself. Sure isn't he my own flesh and blood even if he is poorly furnished upstairs.'

Dad chuckled. 'I wasn't thinkin' of you atin' it. I could just picture it bein' shared out among the cats.'

'I beg your parsnips, y'oul' consequence. I wouldn't do the like a' that with Lulu's nice cake, although now yeh mention it, Susie loved the icing off the cake Mrs. Condell of Blacklion gave me for bein' a good customer. She's very good to me, Mrs. Condell.'

'Oh, I see.' Dad gave her a good-natured shove. 'How well yeh never opened your gob about that before, yeh cuvidgis oul' rip.'

'Heh-Haaargh!'

With the fire blazing in the lads' room it was sheer bliss to climb into bed without shivering and with stomachs agreeably stuffed. It was not unusual for Ray to fall asleep fantasizing about lovely big chunks of bread smothered in thickly spread creamy butter.

But not tonight.

Tonight there was nothing wrong with the world. Nothing at all.

CHAPTER NINE

The ambulance came up the Lane, drove past number fifteen, went on up around the Buildings to turn and in a minute was crunching to a halt at the gate. The apprehensive face that watched it from the kitchen window was almost as white as the dreaded vehicle itself.

This fine October morning in nineteen fifty-three was the most traumatic one in his nine-and-a-half years.

That white terror out there was for him.

He was going into hospital.

'Oh God, Mammy, why do I have to go?'

He asked the question over and over, but only in his head. He didn't want to get Ma going, not now. The ambulance driver pushed the gate open and walked up the path. Ma turned the wireless off, rudely interrupting Johnnie Ray as he walked his baby back home, and opened the door before the man knocked.

'Mornin' Ma'am, is there a lad here for the hospital at Clontarf?'

'Yes, that's right, we're ready. Come on now Raymond.'

He looked longingly out the window at Little Sugarloaf and the Faraway Trees. He quaked inside and his legs felt like the Sunday jelly as he followed Ma out the front door.

Val, Rita and Sheila watched him with a sort of detached curiosity and maybe a touch of excitement at something out of the ordinary taking place. It was half past eight. Dad had gone to work and Mrs. Healy would take care of the younger ones until Ma got home.

He felt the tears well up, gulped hard and blinked them back. After all he was going on ten years of age, the Big Man of the family, and it wouldn't do to break down bawling in front of them all. Val had cried when he went to hospital last year, but then he was only seven and of course the broken leg could have had something to do with it.

Ma was wearing the posh white coat that she reserved for Sundays and special days, smelling of the posh powder that she reserved for exceptional occasions, and chatting to the man in the posh voice reserved for strangers and Jack and Chris.

They sat up front with the driver. There were some other patients in the back who were to be dropped off at various hospitals along the way. Ray was the only one for Clontarf.

Clontarf.

The very word made him shudder. For weeks he had lived in dread of it, while Ma tried to convince him there was nothing to worry about, that it would only be for a week or so.

Janie, did she think he was a flippin' eejit or what? Only the other day in Bray she had been gossiping to Mrs. Ryan and when she thought he was engrossed in a study of the array of sweets in Cullen's window she leaned towards the old lady and whispered with her mouth pulled around to the side of her face:

'Wizza wizza wuzza wuzza operation wizza wuzza.'

Naturally, the one word he wasn't meant to hear was the only one he did hear.

'Ah no, Missus, is that a fact? Ah, sure please God the poor little craythur will be all right.'

This performance was repeated whenever they met anyone who didn't already know. All the futile secrecy fuelled his fear that this operation he was to go under must be a very serious one indeed, and the horror of it had been building up inside him until he wanted to scream at them that he knew all about it, and why couldn't they, especially Ma, just talk to him about it. But he never did, because just thinking of the word 'operation' made him choke and he was afraid that if he actually tried to say it he would start whinging.

Anyway, he was fecked if he could understand why he had to have an operation in the first place. Fallen arches, Ma said. Flat feet. He had never had the slightest bother with his feet, and he was sure there was absolutely nothing wrong with them, any more than there had been anything wrong with his eyes that time when he was in first class. It was as though there were some inexplicable necessity that he should have something the matter with him.

Back then she had hauled him off to an optician who had prescribed some stuff to put in his eyes. Next morning at school he had been horrified to see, for want of a better word, that the blue and red guidelines in his writing copy appeared only as a chaotic blur.

He tried holding the book at arms length and he tried bringing it so close that his nose touched the page, all to no avail.

His teacher at the time was Miss Geraghty, known on account of her luxuriant silvery mane to parents and pupils alike as the Grey Mare. She had larruped the bare thighs off him for his hopeless attempts at writing between the lines, seemingly not finding it in the least strange that this was a sudden complete departure from his usual standard of work.

While he tried to explain that he couldn't see she was slashing away with the cane like one of the Three Musketeers gone mad.

And it was all for nothing.

His sight was perfectly normal and he didn't even get a pair of specs out of the whole episode.

But this was a hundred times worse. They were not going to just rub something into his feet. They were going to cut him open, for God's sake! It all seemed so horribly wrong, like some dreadful mistake he was pathetically powerless to rectify.

The ambulance turned out of the end of the Lane and headed towards Bray. Johnny Wind had been busy last night and shiny conkers littered the road along by the Little Wood. His heart dropped down to his threatened feet as he watched his beloved Ballywaltrim vanish behind him.

The Big Tree where he sometimes sat on the bit of old wall and copied down the numbers of cars that passed, and beside it the two-storied dwelling they called The Yella House, where the Simpson family lived.

Butler's field. Massey Cottage with its thatch golden in the autumn sun. Boghall corner. Darby's Lane.

How long would it be before these scenes gladdened his heart again? If, of course, he ever did see them again.

74

People sometimes died under operations. Hadn't he heard the adults on more than one occasion deplore the untimely passing of some acquaintance who had 'died under the knife'?

Up and over Fairy Hill; past the newly built cottages of Avondale Park; The Soldiers' Road where, coming home from school, they would shout hello to the old World War One veteran who came to sit there in his chain driven wheelchair which he 'pedalled' with his hands. Where the road dipped at Patchwork they passed Mr. Mooney walking out from Bray with his big milk cans and measures delivering the morning milk to customers on the outskirts of the town.

Through the junction of Church and King Edward Roads, where Dad would stop to point out the twinkling lights of Killiney Hill on 'furnace' nights.

Coming to the Town Hall he spotted some of his classmates heading up around the corner to St. Cronan's and for the first time in his life he wished he was going to school, wished that Mr. Donegan, the schoolmaster, was all he had to fear this morning. He swore he would never hate school again.

Sin or no sin, he gazed out fondly at The Divil as they went by. At least it was The Divil he knew, and who knew what class of divil he might have to deal with shortly?

On down the Main Street past Cullen's shop where Dad bought his tobacco and Mr. Cullen would chop the two-ounce bar of Velvan Plug in halves with a dangerous looking half-moon shaped cutter.

Taylor's clock shop where Ma brought the old clock to be repaired, wheeling it in the pram like a baby.

Tom Costello's farmyard.

Doyle's Garage where two of the dads from the lane worked, Dick Carr and Tom Shortt.

Browne's with its thousands of spools of thread in an infinite variety of colours on counters along thickly carpeted aisles, giving the shop a hushed feel and inducing people to speak in subdued tones. Would a bit of carpet on the floor at home have that effect on Ma?

She nudged him with her elbow.

'Bless yourself, we're passin' the church.'

Caprani's the pork butchers with the new all-glass door that Ma had crashed the pram into because she thought there was nothing there.

Caulfield's where the groceries were ordered each week and delivered by Dinny Byrne. He liked going to Caulfield's with Ma. When she paid at the counter the money was put into a little container which was sent zinging along a wire to a small office at the far end of the shop where Miss Reynolds would take it out, pop the change and receipt in its place and send it zinging back down the shop.

He would watch fascinated as the man at the butter counter shaped the big lumps of butter between grooved wooden butter pats, throwing the lumps in the air and never missing one, slapping each lined golden brick onto a sheet of greaseproof paper.

Over Bray Bridge and along by Ravenswell Convent. His eyes darted frantically around the garden hoping to catch a last glimpse of Dad, but he was nowhere to be seen.

Jemmy, Pop, Jimmy, Jamie, Jem; he was given a variety of names by different relations. Ma usually called him Jimmy or sometimes Father, not to mention all the temper-names she bestowed on him.

It didn't matter. Ray believed he was the kindest man that ever was born, and lucky to be alive at all as he had weighed a mere pound and a half at birth on Leap Year Day in nineteen sixteen. His first days on earth were spent in a shoebox that was placed in the oven of the range at their home in St. Kevin's Square, off Main Street. So tiny was he that there was a moment of panic on the occasion of his Christening when he managed to lose himself among the folds of his godmother's voluminous shawl.

Out on the main Dublin road now, he watched the tarmac disappear under the front of the ambulance at an indecent rate, rushing him towards the unknown.

He had recently been to the outpatients' department of the hospital in Merrion Street with Ma and afterwards she had taken him to Stephen's & Bourke's shoe shop to have his feet measured for special boots. He stood on a machine and when he looked in a viewer he could see the bones of his feet in an eerie green light. Then they had gone for a cup of tea in the nearby DBC Tearooms where not only the china but the walls as well were decorated in the blue and white Willow Pattern.

In St. Stephen's Green Ma delighted him by producing a brown paper bag full of breadcrumbs from her message bag for him to throw to the ducks, and he thought how really lovely it was of her to have planned this special treat all along.

That day had been enjoyable enough, but now he had taken a bit of a turn against Dublin. Under present circumstances the city had taken on a rather sinister aura. The huge buildings seemed intimidating and everyone appeared to be rushing somewhere. How anyone could live there permanently was beyond him. Not a field or mountain in sight, and even the buses were twice as high as those around Bray. It was a totally alien world to him, and as distant from Ballywaltrim as he had ever been, except for that one Christmas trip with Aunt Kitty, but that had been so different.

And this place they were taking him to now - this Clontarf - was even farther. His tummy churned.

Ma had lived in Dublin as a little girl. Could that have anything to do with her tempers?

'Isn't he a grand quiet lad,' the driver remarked.

'He is, murrya,' said Ma. 'Just lettin' on to be shy.'

Quiet! He was stricken speechless. Inside he was a cauldron of confusion, boiling over with hundreds of tangled reasons for turning back. He was locked into his own world of fear and dread of what awaited him.

They stopped at the outpatients department and somebody got out of the back. He envied whoever it was; he or she would be going home to somewhere in Wicklow that afternoon.

He prayed to St. Anthony for something to go wrong with the ambulance; for the driver to get lost; for Clontarf to have vanished into thin air when they got to where it was supposed to be.

Ma always said St. Anthony was a great lad to ask a favour of and would never let a body down, but Ray had his doubts. If this chap was so generous how come they were so poor? How come the sandwiches they brought to school were usually spread with dripping or treacle Dad got from the convent kitchen? Not that they weren't devoured greedily.

Ray recalled following a boy who had banana sandwiches around the playground just for the smell. Above all, how come Ma, whose second home was the Church of the Most Holy Redeemer, could only dream of a bit of carpet. His own dream was to grow up and become rich enough to buy her a carpet for every room in the house, but if Ma was right about his future prospects it wasn't very likely to come true.

The driver jumped back into his seat and cheerfully announced that they hadn't far to go now as if it were good news.

About ten minutes later they drove up a tree-lined avenue and pulled up in front of a big house that reminded him of Ballymorris House opposite the end of the Lane back home.

This was it. The Orthopaedic Hospital.

There was no escape now, and St. Anthony obviously didn't give a shite what happened to him. Inside, a sister took some particulars and while she was talking with Ma a nurse approached and said to come along now Raymond

He managed a whimpered goodbye to Ma, who said she would see him in a few days, and followed the nurse up a stairway. She led him into a bathroom and told him to take all his clothes off. He nearly died at the thought of stripping off to his bare skin in the presence of a complete stranger, but did as she asked, fumbling and stumbling as he stepped out of his pants.

'In you go,' she said, pushing him towards the steaming water.

He stepped into a real bath for the first time in his life and the nurse washed him. It was a superfluous exercise as Ma had all but scrubbed the skin off him last night. He was grateful when the nurse handed him a towel and told him to dry himself. Ma would drive the corner of the towel into your ear like a corkscrew until you yelped, earning yourself a puck on the side of the head that gave you bells in your ears.

'Stand still, fool!'

There was no bathroom at home. On Saturday nights the old zinc tub was placed in front of the range and filled with kettles and pots of hot water, and everybody wanted to be first in while the water was unpolluted and warm.

Dad's sister Aunt Sarah and Uncle Paddy had called one night along with young Declan and Cathy when Ray was in the bath, and Ma never allowed her Saturday night schedule to be disrupted or delayed by anybody.

'Stand up,' she ordered.

'Ah, Mam...'

'Stand up, fathead, and don't be bloody ridiculous.'

She gave him a wallop that threatened to send him sizzling like a wet sausage onto the red-hot range. Ma's orders, like those of the Martian in 'Journey into Space', were to be 'obeyed without question at all times'.

The nurse went off with his clothes and came back a few minutes later with an armful of hospital clothes.

'You can put these on. I've given your own things to your mother to bring home.'

Everything, shirt, pants, pullover and socks, was grey.

Not being allowed to wear his own clothes was something he hadn't thought of and he hated the idea. As he got dressed he wallowed in self-pity and wondered why everything seemed to be carefully planned to ensure that his misery was as deep as possible.

He noticed they had left him his own boots. That itself. Those boots had left their prints in special places.

She brought him to a room with the word 'Quarantine' on the door, and having shown him his allotted bed, she left him.

Not knowing what, if anything, he was supposed to do, he stood by the bed and surveyed the other beds around the ward. Each held a small boy or girl looking as wide-eyed and frightened as he himself felt, and from a bed in a corner weak whimpering sounds came from an unseen patient.

A different nurse appeared with a tray of dinners. He was given one but could only pick at it. It was followed by a big dollop of sago with two tablets stuck in it, one white like an Aspro, the other a round rubbery capsule. He managed to swallow them with a small amount of sago but his stomach heaved violently. The sago was slimy, not at all the way Ma made it. When the nurse returned the dish was still full.

'Oh, now now! What's this? We must eat our sweet. After all, we only ate half of our dinner, didn't we?'

She kept saying 'we' but there was no sign of her having a go at the revolting frogspawn herself. Such a quare way to talk! He longed for Ballywaltrim where people could talk right. She took a spoonful and held it to his mouth. He opened and swallowed.

'There we are!' she said.

He heaved even more violently this time and we seemed to get the message. Realizing we were in eminent danger of getting it back in our face we just said 'Now now!' again and 'Tut tut' and took ourselves off, frogspawn and all.

His first night in hospital was a haunting experience. He got into bed around seven o'clock and lay there visualizing what might be going on at home. Dad would be home from work and they would all be sitting around the range, probably talking about Ray. Maybe Val would be gone out for swaps with a bundle of comics under his oxter.

Oh, Holy God! Just to be going out for swaps tonight.

'Any swaps?' was the cry at each cottage door as it was opened in answer to knock or yodel.

'Yeah, but I've only got Dells an' I'll be wantin' two of them Eagles or Toppers for each. Right?'

'OK, giz a look then.'

The only place they ventured to beyond the cottages was Ballywaltrim House where Oliver O'Farrell usually had a good supply of comics, but there was a dark and lonely stretch of road between the end of the Lane and his home at the corner of Ballywaltrim Lane, and Westmoreland, the haunted house, had to be passed on the way. It stood only a few hundred yards from the road, up a dark winding avenue, and what was a few hundred yards to a ghost?

This short excursion was seldom undertaken at night except in pairs, but he had chanced it alone one stormy night when he found he had exhausted all available reading matter in the Lane. When Mrs. O'Farrell opened the door and he thankfully entered the lighted glass porch he had wanted to ask her if he could stay the night, so frightful had been his imaginings as he had tiptoed up along the middle of the road, and not a solitary car had come along to help light his way.

Ten minutes hard bargaining with Oliver and then a frantic dash back down the road, not daring to stop or look back until he was under the friendly glow of the bottom light, the Big Tree shrieking nearby in the gale.

Never again, he had vowed. Not for a dozen Captain Marvels.

'Young f'la.'

His fond musing was interrupted by a pathetically weak cry from the bed in the corner.

Nobody replied.

'Young f'la.'

Again no response. He wondered which 'young f'la' the plaintive voice was endeavouring to make contact with. Every few minutes the pitiful cries were repeated and after about half an hour it occurred to him that maybe the owner of the voice had seen him come into the ward, the last patient to do so, and that he, Ray, might very well be the 'young f'la' for whom the pleading calls were intended.

'Young f'la,' followed by a whimper.

He decided to answer and find out one way or the other.

'Yes?'

It was one of the very few words he had uttered since his arrival.

'Wah-teh, wah-teh, young f'la.'

Now what the flames did that mean.

'Pardon?'

'Wah-teh.'

He tried to puzzle it out.

'Young f'la.'

'What?'

'Wah-teh, drink wah-teh.'

It sounded like it took a terrific effort and trailed off into a heartbreaking wail.

Water! The poor little divil wanted a drink of water. Ah, God.

He wondered what the child's ailment was; what he looked like - if indeed he was a he - and how it was he came to be so desperately thirsty. He must be really ill, Ray thought, if he can't even look out of his bed.

And what could Ray do?

He was too frightened himself to say a word to anyone. The hours crawled by, sleep impossible with his mind so full of foreboding, and from the corner the piteous pleading for a drink of water went on and on. During the night a nurse looked in now and then but never seemed to hear the small voice calling.

Maybe because of his complaint, whatever it was, he wasn't allowed drink water.

In the morning a boy of around his own age poked his head around the door. Most of the children were still sleeping and his gaze travelled from bed to bed until he saw Ray lying awake.

'Howiyeh?' he said in a sharp little hard man's voice.

'Good!' Ray replied, not by way of describing his condition, but using the Ballywaltrim vernacular for 'Hello', 'Good morning', or even 'Howiyeh?'

'What's yer name?' the lad asked, grinning cheekily all over his face as he sauntered over to the bedside. He looked to Ray the kind of fellow who would chance anything, but he liked him straight away.

'Raymond Cranley,' he informed him.

'Jaysus, that's a quare one! Where do yeh live?'

'In Bray.'

The boy's eyes widened and he whistled through his teeth and said 'Jaysus!' again.

'That's down the country in the middle a' nowhere, isn't it? I live in Cabra, Jimmy Reilly's me name. Do yeh live in one of them houses with straw on the roof?'

At that moment in Ray's life Bray was Paradise, and no little Jackeen was going to get away with any derogatory remarks about his beloved hometown.

'No, I don't. There's twenty five houses on our lane and none of them is thatched. There's only a few thatched houses around Bray. It's a great place to live.'

'An' do yeh live in the town itself?'

'No. About a mile on the Wicklow side of it.'

Jimmy whistled again.

'Gorny, yeh really are a culchie then, aren't yeh? A Wickla goatsucker!'

These were new definitions of his roots to Ray and he wasn't sure what to make of them, so he just replied that he would rather live out there than in the city any day.

'Gerraway, sure what's out there on'y trees an' fields an' mountains.'

'We have two picture houses in Bray.'

'Yiz have?'

'Yeah, the Royal an' the Roxy. The seats in the Roxy are always collapsin' under yeh. Ma calls it the flea-bank, but it's only fourpence to get into the pit there. It's sixpence in the Royal.'

'Who's yer favourah?'

'Hopalong Cassidy.'

'Nah, he's stupah. Royal Rogers is my favourah. He's the king idda cowboys.'

With this he drew his six-gun, shot the light out and wiped out half the ward before nonchalantly blowing the smoke from the barrels of his weapons and re-holstering them.

'Royal Rogers id fill Cassidy fulla lead 'fore he could clear leather,' he cockily proclaimed his hero's invincibility.

Ray was getting into the swing of it now, temporarily forgetting his woes in the company of this little hardchaw.

'At least Hoppy doesn't go around singin' to his horse like a big sissy,' he retorted.

Jimmy changed the subject.

'What are yeh in here for anyway?'

'It's me feet. I have to have an operation.'

'So have I. I had one foot done last year an' I'm back now to get the other done.'

'What's it like? Does it hurt?'

'Not while they're doin' it, it doesn't. They put yeh asleep an' yeh wake up with yer leg in plaster, an' then the pain id fuckin' kill yeh. But the worst is the enema.'

'The what?'

'The enema.'

'What's that?'

'Ooh Jaysus, it's on'y feckin' awful. They stick a tube up yer arse an' pour a big jug a' stuff up yeh.'

Oh Mammy, no! A new wave of terror swept over him.

'What do they do that for?' he asked, hoping it was something to do with other people, not him.

'It's to make yeh shite an' clean yer belly out. Everyone gets it the day before they get the knife.'

He laughed his hard man's laugh at Ray's obvious horror.

'I berra go,' he said, and went swaggering down the landing singing at the top of his voice his Cabra version of Strauss's 'Blue Danube'.

'It's all on yer leg, gick-gick, la-la.

It's three inches thick, gick-gick, la-la.

It's hard as a brick, gick-gick, la-la.

It's lovely to lick, gick-gick, la-la...'

Next day Ray was taken into another room, stripped naked and told to stand on a box the size of an orange crate over which a black cloth that covered the wall behind it was draped. A man stood behind a tripod that held a large camera. They're going to take my picture with nothing on! Oh, Mammy, what sort of place have you sent me to at all? This has to be a mortal sin. He shivered in his misery. The nurse told him to keep his hands by his sides and his chin up. He looked longingly at the heavily curtained window opposite him and wished he had the powers of Captain Marvel, who only had to say 'Shazam!' and he could take off and fly there and then. No waiting to change clothes like that slowcoach Superman. Not that Ray, given his present situation, would have to worry about clothes one way or the other.

He pictured himself crashing through the window, leaving nurse and photographer dumbfounded as he soared over Dublin and headed for home, his guiding beacon the graceful cone of the Great Sugarloaf.

Wild, wonderful Wicklow.

He wouldn't go to his house though. No. They would only send him back. Darley's barn would be just the job. He would be safe there where he and his pals had often buried themselves in the hay for warmth on winter days, or on other occasions to hide from Mr. Lawlor as he passed on his way home to the gate lodge. A few minutes under the hay and you were soaking with sweat, your nostrils full of hay-dust and body itching maddeningly from the attentions of the myriad forms of hopping, crawling life that inhabited the barn.

None of these minor discomforts would bother him in the slightest. He would be snug enough.

And it was October; the pears in Darley's orchard would be ripe and accessible, hanging like big juicy drops on the garden wall, and he could throw 'weapons' into the great walnut tree on the front avenue to bring showers of the green-jacketed nuts down around him.

He would give Ronnie Turner a yodel from the wood. Ronnie would keep him company in the daytime and wouldn't tell.

Yes, but what about night-time?

The grand plan was suddenly scuppered when he remembered that the barn was only yards from Westmoreland, derelict since Murphy's had moved to their new bungalow, Stella Maris, on the main road beside Andy's. It had been a friendly old house when Murphy's were in residence and he had often sat on the sunny steps while Ma gossiped with Mrs. Murphy.

It was so different now; a soulless dead place, hardly a pane of glass left intact, its great doorway agape in a horrible black howl. He had heard from some of the older boys who claimed to have ventured inside that the toes of a pair of Wellington boots could be seen protruding from under a wall in one of the upstairs rooms. Obviously some old farmer had been murdered and walled up in there, and his was the spook that haunted the place. The thumping noises that were reputedly heard coming from the house after dark were probably caused by the wellies on the bare stairs and landings as he clumped around looking for his killer, seeking revenge.

And who is to say he didn't pop outside now and again to check out the barn? The ghost of a chap whose life has been violently terminated by one of his fellows is apt to be a little on the cranky side, and if a lad was discovered by such a fetch, sleeping in his barn, he might find himself rudely awakened by a spooky root up the posterior administered by a ghostly wellie.

It was one thing playing around the place with a gang of your pals in broad daylight, quite another by yourself at night. He would have to think of something else.

The camera flashed.

He whispered 'Shazam!' through clenched teeth.

Nothing happened.

CHAPTER TEN

He was mortified. Never in his life had he felt so ashamed. Here he lay in a strange bed with his face buried in the pillow and his bum in the air while a severe-looking sister held the cheeks of his bottom apart with one hand and pushed a cold tube into him with the other, her lips pursed and eyes squinting in concentration.

He turned his face and saw a nurse pour the contents of a jug into a funnel at the top of the tube. The sister picked up a white enamelled bedpan.

'Be ready to turn around quickly and sit on this when the nurse has finished,' she ordered stiffly.

At first he didn't notice much, then a slight feeling of wanting to go to the lav, changing as the nurse poured to a more urgent feeling of wanting to go, and, as the jug emptied, to an impossibly irresistible feeling of wanting to go. He was convinced that as soon as the tube was removed he would go scuttering around the ward like a deflating balloon.

'Now!' the sister shouted.

She stuck the bedpan under him as he twirled himself around, desperately trying to control the cruel urge to let go. The din when the deluge hit the bedpan was similar to that of a downpour of hailstones on a galvanised iron foot. He reddened at the sniggers of some of the kids. He was glad Jimmy Reilly was still unconscious in the next bed. Jimmy would have laughed his head off. He had had his op that morning.

Ray had been moved from Quarantine to 'the butcher's waiting room', Jimmy's title for the ward where children were prepared for the theatre and stayed for their immediate post-operative care. Later they would be shifted to a place called the veranda to recuperate, which, if Jimmy was to be believed, took some months.

Months! He was afraid to let himself think about it.

When the sister and nurse had gone he lay back exhausted and looked over at Jimmy. Something protruded from between his lips.

'It's to prevent him from biting his tongue,' said Michael O'Connell from his bed at the opposite side of the ward.

Michael wasn't a bit like Jimmy, although he too was a Dubliner. He spoke quietly and well, and was of a gentler disposition. He lived in Homefarm Park on the north side of the city and his dad had a car, so they were obviously very rich.

Jimmy began to move in the bed and was moaning. His eyes suddenly flew open and the thing popped out of his mouth followed by a stream of watery looking stuff.

'Ooh Jaysus fuck, I'm sick!' were the first words he uttered.

Janie, he's an awful curser, Ray thought. Did he not worry that he might die during the operation with a mortal sin on his soul and be roasted and tortured in hell for all eternity, the Divil paying special attention to his tongue with a red-hot poker?

Some curses were only venial sins, like feck, bloody and shite, but fuck, Jaysus, cunt and bollix were mortalers and Jimmy spouted them all with gusto.

Ray dreaded the thought of Ma ever dropping dead during a temper. She wouldn't have a hope. Or would she? After all, she only cursed when she was in a temper, and that was usually the fault of Dad or the kids, so maybe she would be forgiven and the rest of the family would be condemned to oul' Nick's hob for the attempted damnation of her immortal soul.

Sometimes Ma would pick a particular curse-word and would go through several tempers using mainly that one expletive. In the warm-up to a temper she would go about the house banging the sweeping brush on doors and furniture muttering 'Cunts!' or 'Whores!' or whatever the flavour of the week happened to be, and that title would be accorded to male, female, young and old alike.

But she drew the line at bollix. She never used that one, and if Ma refrained from including it in her awesome curse-word vocabulary then it was safe to assume that the word was the deadliest of mortalers, as Val found out one day to his cost. He and some of the kids had been listening as Jimmy Jones from number eleven entertained them with some tunes on his mouth organ on the lane. The instrument had let him down in mid-performance and Jimmy gave up in disgust, explaining to his young fans that the mouth organ was bollixed.

Val lost no time in running home to tell Ma about the strange-sounding misfortune that had overtaken the harmonica. As soon as the word passed his lips he was amazed to see Ma coming at him, arms flailing like a windmill.

If the Divil tried to roast Ma she would probably run him out of hell.

It was Ray's turn for the theatre, or as Jimmy would have it, the tee-ay-tor. He was given two injections and wheeled into the evil-smelling place. Somebody held a mask over his face and said 'Deep breaths now'. A moment of panic, white-masked faces swimming over him, and then he was waking up as sick as a dog.

A wire cage had been placed under the covers to keep the weight off his leg, which was now transmitting dull painful signals to his brain. Jimmy Reilly looked across at him sympathetically.

'Howiyeh? It's awful when yeh wake up at first, isn't it? Yid think yeh were fuckin'-well dyin''

Ray didn't answer, couldn't answer. His mouth and throat felt as if they had been given a good going over with a rasp, and his whole body felt like a horse had fallen on it. Jimmy said he had spat the 'thingamerry' out of his mouth before regaining consciousness. The day passed in a state of hazy semi-awareness. They gave him some tea and toast in the evening. The tea was heaven and he found that after drinking it he could talk a bit to Jimmy.

The pain in his leg now throbbed like a massive toothache, and sleep was almost impossible. Long after the rest of the ward had dropped off Jimmy and himself were still talking.

'Yeh berra gerra birra sleep,' Jimmy yawned eventually, 'yeh won't feel so bad tomorrah.'

When Ray spoke to him a few minutes later there was no response. Alone now, he let his thoughts drift and finally dozed off only to be awakened again by sounds in the ward. The noises came from a bed that stood upon a raised platform at the back of the ward. Its occupant was a boy, Joe, much older than any of the others. Around sixteen, Ray guessed, but he never spoke and only changed his position in the bed when the nurses rolled him onto one side or the other.

Early that morning, before Ray had been carted off to theatre, the ward had been treated to the spectacle of a nurse shaving a mass of black hair from around Joe's genitals. As she got on with the job Joe suddenly gave a loud grunt and the nurse jumped back, knocking her chair over and sending a basin of soapy water flying. A younger nurse who had been helping held her hand over her mouth as tears of suppressed laughter streamed down her face.

Jimmy, back to his old self by then, remarked: 'Gorny, did yeh see the size idda prick on yer man?'

Another new word for Ray. In Ballywaltrim it was a mickey.

'Yeah,' he replied, 'but what happened?'

'Did yeh not see? It went all over the feckin' nurse,' he chortled.

'I thought it was suds from the basin,' Ray replied, and Jimmy laughed even louder.

'He does it hisself sometimes, so he does. He used to do it when I was here last year too. I think it's somethin' to do with what ails him, yeh know.'

Now in the darkened ward at God knew what hour of the night, Joe was obviously 'doin' it hisself again'.

'So now!' said Ma leaving a brown paper bag on his bed. 'Aren't yeh glad you're over yer big operation?'

Operation! Well holy flippin' God. It was the first time she had admitted to him that such a thing was even a remote possibility.

'There's a few sweets for yeh, an' a couple of apples, an' some comics Val sent in.'

'Thanks. Will I be home for Christmas?'

'A-course yeh will, sure that's weeks away yet. Anyway, it's great in hospital at Christmas, they do have grand parties an' all.'

His fears were confirmed. He had as much hope of being home for Christmas as Ma had of winning the Fifty.

The Fifty was the top prize of fifty pounds in the Bray Silver Circle Non-stop Draw, for which she purchased a one-shilling ticket each week from Maggie Crinnion, only to have 'some oul' shagger that's rollin' in it' win every time. The mind-boggling sum of fifty pounds would change the standard of living at number fifteen beyond recognition. Anyone who won the Fifty never looked back.

Visiting time over, Ma said:

'I'll send yer oul' lad in to see yeh next week. I'll have to write out the numbers of the buses for him. God knows where the hell he'll end up.'

But Dad arrived safe and sound the following Sunday. Tears shone in his eyes as he approached the bed, and Ray's own eyes filled up as Dad gave him one of his Sunday kisses, a different class of kiss altogether from his weekday one which the drowsy-eyed kids usually awoke to in the mornings before he left for work, his stubbly chin rubbing playfully against their cheeks, while Ma stood waiting for her birdie in the front hall where he kept his bike.

Today, however, was Sunday, and on Sundays Dad was a dapper cross between Clark Gable and David Niven; moustache neatly trimmed, chin smooth-shaven, hair immaculately groomed and smelling sweetly of come-back.

'Well son, how are yeh, God love yeh?' he said with a bit of a snuffle.

'All right, but I'd rather be at home, Daddy.'

'A-course yeh would, but sure please God yeh won't be here too long.'

'I hope not. D'yeh go to the furnace every night now?'

'I do. Sure I'm run off me feet. I do har'ly be able to put a foot under me be the time I'm finished at night. I do be bet. But don't worry, yeh'll be comin' with me again in no time at all.'

He listened eagerly as Dad related all the goings on at home to him until a nurse rang the little bell that signalled the end of visiting time. Dad took out his pipe.

'I better stoke up this oul' furnace now, an' go in the name a' God. One of us'll see yeh next week.'

He threw his top coat over his left arm, his hat gripped in three fingers of the same hand, leaned over holding the pipe to one side in the other and, with eyes brimming again, kissed Ray goodbye.

At the door he turned to wave and collided with a nurse coming in. Sparks and apologies flew profusely. He looked back, threw his eyes up with an embarrassed grin, waved again and was gone, leaving the ward empty of anything that mattered.

Trying to make up his mind whether to laugh or cry he decided that the collision with the nurse was comical and laughed, but the tears came anyway.

'I got bananas!' Jimmy boasted later, holding up a golden bunch for inspection. 'D'yeh wanta swap somethin'?'

Ray looked in the bag Dad had brought. Those bananas looked delicious.

'I'll give yeh half a packet of Fruit Gums for a banana,' he offered hopefully.

'Is it the shites, now, or the heartburn yeh have? Gimme the whole packet.'

'But that's all I have,' Ray protested.

'I'll tell yeh what, I'll give yeh one ouva the packet then,' Jimmy offered big-heartedly.

His generosity swung the balance. Ray handed over his packet of sweets and received one back before Jimmy broke the smallest banana from the bunch. Ray polished it off in seconds. Jimmy was still chewing gums an hour later.

He was a quare eel and would in all probability grow up to be an oul' bester.

One thing Ray didn't miss about home was senna. Saturday was senna day. In the morning Ma would pour hot water on the dreaded pods and make a pot of the most vilely nauseating 'tea' imaginable. Stomachs heaved as the fumes assailed nostrils in a sickening reminder of horrors to come.

It took enormous willpower to resist throwing up while trying to drink the foul brew, and then you waited, close to home, for your insides to go into uproar and double you up with great rolling cramps. Afterwards you felt weak, light-headed and ravenous, and wondered why it was necessary to have your stomach scoured out regularly when there wouldn't be a whole lot in it anyway.

CHAPTER ELEVEN

It was coming up to Christmas and he was getting around on crutches, but his foot was still extremely painful if he accidentally let it touch the floor. He had been shifted out to the veranda, down a narrow sloping passageway that connected it to the older main hospital building. At the end of the long passage the boys' veranda consisted of an L-shaped wing to the left, while the girls occupied the wing to the right. A small office opposite the end of the passage divided the two wings.

His bed was halfway along the foot of the L and he could see the girls' veranda across an open rectangle of lawn. It was good to see even that small stretch of grass. The glass doors that fronted the veranda were opened right back most days giving the youngsters all the benefits of outdoor living in the depths of an Irish winter.

On Sundays he sat on his bed and watched for Ma's white coat among the stream of visitors emerging from the sloping passage, and he would give a little involuntary cry of joy as she appeared coming around by the office towards him with all the news of home. He hadn't seen her in a temper in almost two months and that was wonderful, but at the same time he knew he would gladly put up with anything in the way of ructions at home if he could just be there.

Dad came to visit him about one week in four. He loved Dad more than anything in the world.

Every morning at around six o'clock he was awakened by a nurse and given a cup of cold milk and a chunk of bread and butter. In his drowsy state the milk stopped his breath and made him gasp noisily, the sound repeated along the line of beds as all the boys dealt with this sudden shock to their sleepy systems.

Until now six o'clock in the morning had been a time he had only heard about, an unknown world inhabited in his imagination by shadowy farmers milking cows in fields still cloaked in pre-dawn darkness.

It was an unnatural hour for a boy to be awake.

A couple of days before Christmas he was given a haircut by Paddy, one of the two handymen at the hospital, and he wished he was sitting in Jemmy Doran's barber's shop in the tiny Victorian cottage at Church Terrace, where the walls were adorned with pictures of film stars extolling the virtues of various hair preparations, and Jemmy nearly shaking the brains out of his head as he rubbed the come-back in when the job was finished.

The two lads had given Dad a hard time the day he had taken them for their first haircut, creating such a racket at Jemmy Doran's that he had hauled them back up the town, locks intact, to where he persuaded them there practiced a nicer barber, a Mr. Dornin, whose place of work was at the back of a little sweet-shop which he also owned. With some toothsome bribe from the shop promised on completion of the job they marched bravely in through the front section, but on opening the door to the barber's room they beheld all the haircutting paraphernalia similar to that at Doran's and the bawling recommenced.

Retreating hastily a second time Dad figured that their only hope now was old George Hannon who lived near Aunt Sarah in Wolfe Tone Square, and who might cut their hair in his own house, and there in the less intimidating surroundings of George's small living room they finally had

101

their locks shorn for the first time. Since then they had gone to Jemmy Doran's without fuss.

The second handyman at the hospital was Christy, a smaller man than paddy, who liked to rub his stubbly chin against the children's faces for fun, reminding Ray of Dad. Some of the older boys said Christy was Santy, but Ray and the younger ones knew that this could not be so as Santy didn't even live in Ireland.

A portable screen was set up in the Quarantine ward and they were treated to a film version of 'Gulliver's Travels'. Ray thoroughly enjoyed this as it was a change from the usual cowboy and Indian films that made up ninety per cent of the films shown in the Royal and Roxy. He sat fascinated as the giant Gulliver picked his way carefully among the Lilliputians saying: 'My, my, my!'

Christmas away from home was made a little more tolerable by lots of extra visitors. He saw Val for the first time in months, looking as fine as fippence, all rigged out in his best clothes, hair shining with come-back, and the tops of his socks turned neatly down over the white elastic garters Ma made to stop their socks from falling down around their ankles.

'I got a loada swaps for yeh,' he said, handing Ray a bundle of comics.

Aunts Sarah and Kitty came to see him, and cousin Marie. Kitty sang 'The Golden Vanity' and he nearly cried when he thought about Windgates and their walks down Ennis's Lane to the sea.

When the festive season was over he found himself more homesick than ever.

He became quite accomplished on the crutches, and crutch racing along the veranda was a popular pastime among those fit enough to take part. Now that his foot didn't hurt so badly he could fairly fly along by the beds. These races were frowned upon by the sisters, but most of the nurses turned a blind eye.

One day as he raced some boys to the angle of the veranda somebody shot him.

Luckily the hospital trousers were of heavy material and the lead pellet failed to penetrate, but bejakers did it sting! And it left an angry bruise that had him sitting half on and half off his chair for more than a week. Several of the lads on the veranda had airguns but he never found out the culprit's identity. Some of the bigger boys at home had pellet guns too, and used them to shoot birds and rats. The guns could be bought in Owens's toyshop in Bray, where they were on display among the Dinkie toys and model aeroplanes in the window.

Towards the end of January he was taken to the little office where the plaster was cut from his leg with an electric saw which sported a tiny lethal-looking circular blade. He held his breath as the saw whined a fraction of an inch from his skin, certain that at any second his leg would be sliced open again, this time without the alleviating effects of an anaesthetic.

When the plaster was removed his leg felt as light as a dry traneen, and sharp stabbing pains resulted from attempts to put his weight on it. An ugly raw-looking scar ran from the side of his big toe up under his ankle and to his lower calf. He was brought back to the photographer and once again stood naked and shivering as he waited for the blinding flash. He didn't bother saying 'Shazam!' this time.

This photo was later placed beside the earlier one on the chart that hung on the end of his bed. He wondered why it was that in both photographs his mickey had been scribbled out. He asked Ma about it one day and from the look she gave him he knew that he was a very lucky lad to be in hospital at that particular moment.

Mickies must be a sin to look at.

The hospital gym was situated halfway up the sloping passage and with his weak and thin leg he made his way there every day. A tall old lady, called Miss Greene by the nurses and Lizzie by the kids, slowly got him walking without crutches again. The exercises became gradually less painful until with the aid of 'steels' - two steel bars that went from the heel of his boot to just below the knee on each side of his leg where they terminated in an encircling leather-covered strap - he could get around quite normally.

On one occasion the unfortunate immobile Joe from the ward upstairs was wheeled into the gym and placed on a table. He was naked except for a large net that enveloped him, head and all, like a trapped wild animal in a Tarzan film.

A doctor pointed and probed at various parts of his body with a stick as if Joe was nothing, while a group of younger doctors and nurses looked on, nodding and muttering and taking notes. It was a strange and disturbing sight and Ray hoped it was not something that might be in store for himself.

He thought of the kittens Aunt Kitty would put into a nylon stocking before drowning them in the water barrel at the side of the house.

CHAPTER TWELVE

In the late night stillness Nurse Blakely's footsteps echoed down the veranda as she left the office and walked along by the beds, pausing to glance at each sleeping occupant as she passed.

Ray was awake. He was glad Nurse Blakely was on duty tonight; she was very friendly and often chatted with him for what seemed like hours but in reality was probably much less, until he fell asleep. She was tall and slim with a luxuriant crop of black hair that billowed out from under her nurse's cap.

She couldn't have been more different from Nurse West who had been on duty the night before. Nurse West was about four feet two tall and of similar girth, and Jimmy had once rather picturesquely remarked:

'I'd say that one 'id walk away from a quare shite!'

Whenever she was on nights Ray pretended to be asleep because she hadn't been too pleased when she came around on a couple of occasions and found him awake.

He looked up and smiled as Nurse Blakely came up to his bed.

'So,' she said quietly, 'naughty Raymond's awake again. Dreaming of this wonderful Bray place of his, no doubt.'

She laughed and sat herself down on the side of the bed. As they talked he became aware that she seemed different somehow to-night, her remarks as he prattled on seeming to be vague and having no relevance to what he was saying, as if her mind was off somewhere else.

Then, for no reason he could think of, she leaned over him, her hair tickling his face, and kissed his forehead.

'You're a lovely boy, aren't you?' she whispered.

He didn't reply and it didn't seem to matter to her.

'Are you my boy? Do you think I'm nice?'

She was breathing all funny. He nodded into her hair.

She moved herself around until she was lying full length on the bed. As slender as she was she felt heavy on his skinny ten-year-old frame. She began rotating the lower half of her body against his bony pelvis, her chest level with his face.

He turned his head sideways so he could breathe.

What the flames was she doing? Was there something the matter with her? What could have come over her all of a slap?

And she kept talking quare, all yes, yes, and beautiful, beautiful and stuff like that. He was fecked if he could see anything that could be the cause of such breathless excitement, although he thought she smelled lovely in her crispy-fresh uniform.

She was pounding her body hard against him now, each thump driven home with a guttural 'Jesus!'

He became a little alarmed. This was nice Nurse Blakely, always so friendly and happy. What was happening to her at all?

She plunged her face into the pillow above his head to stifle her cries, nearly smothering him against her chest.

Suddenly the truth, what had to be the truth, flashed upon him.

She's dying!

Of course! That was it! That's why she kept saying Jesus. Didn't Mr. Donegan tell the class at school a while back that they should endeavour to let their last dying word be Jesus, so that they would go to meet their Maker with the Saviour's name on their lips?

Oh Godjesusmammy help me she's dying. She'll die on top of me and smother me.

He could feel as well as hear the strange convulsions in her throat as she gasped her weird strangled cries into the pillow. He thought she was going to drive him through the bed as her lower body slammed against him frenziedly, then he felt her go all floppy and still.

She's dead! Mammy get me outa here, she's…

He was about to let a panic-stricken yell out of him when he realized she was still breathing.

'There now, it's all right, lovey. It's all right now.'

She lifted her head and her face was flushed as if she had been crying.

'Off you go to sleep now, Raymond. I'll come and chat to you tomorrow night again.'

He was flabbergasted. Holy God almighty, here she was talking to him in her usual kindly way as if that terrible attack she had just gone through had never happened. It was the quarest thing he had ever come across. Maybe she would be all right tomorrow night; maybe it would never happen to her again, whatever it was.

But it did.

She took the very same sort of turn the following night, and regularly after that until he became accustomed to it and it didn't bother him anymore. The strangest thing about it was that she seemed to actually like it happening.

Some instinct told him he shouldn't say anything to Ma about this, so he sang dumb.

He had told her about Bridie Daly all right. Bridie was his girlfriend on the girls' veranda, and every evening before bed he would venture across the grass to the back of the office where he would give her a peck on the cheek, after which they would both run back to their respective verandas chased by a gang of chanting hard-chaws.

'We're goin' ta tell

You rang the bell

Yeh kissed yer mot

Yeh should be shot

An' chucked inta hell!'

Ma did not approve of Bridie. She gave him the same look she had given him when he had asked her about his nude photograph, but what connection there could possibly be between girlfriends and mickies he hadn't a clue.

CHAPTER THIRTEEN

During that long winter in hospital he discovered that comics were anything but the ultimate in reading material. He had derived such great pleasure from them up until now that he would have found it difficult to believe there could be something better. Books had always looked boring to him. Page after page of monotonous print unrelieved by brightly coloured pictures, or even black and white ones.

He didn't know how adults could be bothered sitting around for hours trying to get through such seemingly uninteresting tomes.

As he wandered from bed to bed one day in search of a comic he hadn't read, an older boy offered him a fairly thick hardback book, assuring him that it was a really pippy story and urging him to at least have a go at reading it.

Ray took the volume back to his bed and, lying on his tummy with his hands under his chin and the pillow acting as a book-rest, he began to read Robinson Crusoe.

Within minutes he was hooked. He spent the best part of a week in the fascinating company of Defoe's shipwrecked hero on his lonely island. When he finished he went back to the beginning and read it all through again. He closed it the second time convinced that his comic-reading days were over.

There was a children's library in Bray. When he got home he would save all his pennies until he had the necessary shilling to join, and he couldn't wait to tell the lads back home that books had stories better than any comic.

Comics were an island, books the rest of the world. Robinson Crusoe had rescued him.

When 'Hospitals Requests' was on the wireless those patients capable of leaving their beds gathered in the office to listen, and one day in February a song called 'Don't Sell Daddy Any More Whiskey' was played for Ray as a birthday request from the rest of the family. It was a number Ma had taken to singing around the house when in good form, and an odd choice, it being highly unlikely that Dad had ever had the price of a whiskey to spare in his life.

Word came down from the wards that little Eddie, whose pleas for a drink of water had troubled Ray on his first night in hospital, was dead. He wondered if the poor little divil ever got that drink, or had he died for the want of it.

The days lengthened and the milk in the mornings seemed less icy as the weather became gradually warmer. He was delighted to find that a boy a few beds away, Gerry Devitt, was from Bray. They had never met at home and it was only when Dad recognized his parents on visiting day that Gerry was introduced. It was good to talk with someone who was familiar with the places he missed so much.

The doctor, on his weekly round, got Ray to walk up and down, sat him on the bed and twisted his foot this way and that, hummed and hawed, rubbed his chin and the shiny dome of his head and walked on to the next bed, speaking in low tones to the sister and nurse who accompanied him. What's he saying about me? Why do they have to bloomin'-well whisper all the time?

He knew the time could not be far away when he would be for the knife again, an event that he would gladly have postponed until the sun came up on Galway Bay.

On his way back along the veranda Doctor Fitzgerald - 'Fitzer' to the patients - addressed him directly for the first time.

'Well, Raymond, we can go ahead with number two soon. The right one is coming along fine. However, we'll give you a break first. You may go home for a month. All right?'

He couldn't believe what he was hearing.

Home!

He nearly nodded his head off as his heart rose on a flood of joy. A month, a day, an hour, it didn't matter tuppence. He was going to see Ballywaltrim again. Somehow over the months he had become resigned to an indefinite stay in hospital, and while home constantly loomed large in his mind, hope of getting there did not.

He skipped and danced along the line of beds spreading the glad tidings up and down the veranda.

'Well, there's no dowra bowra, yer a lucky fucker,' Jimmy said. 'It shubby me goin' home first, an' me with me op done before yeh. Just think! No more feckin' sago. No more freezin' milk at all hours idda mornin'. Yer on'y steeped, so yeh are.'

The night before he was due to go home Nurse Blakely, having performed her usual ritual, went all soppy like the mots in the pictures, saying how terribly she was going to miss him and what was she going to do at all without her little friend, and how glad she was that he would be back in a month and she would go mad waiting.

Ray, for his part, although she was undeniably his favourite nurse, couldn't have cared less if he never clapped eyes on her again, and fervently hoped that things would in

112

fact turn out that way. He couldn't understand why she was being such a fusspot about it anyway; wasn't the place full of lads she could lie on top of?

He kissed Bridie Daly behind the office for the last time and watched her limp back to the girls' veranda and out of his life. Love is a quare thing when you're ten. He would love her forever and ever, of course, but Ballywaltrim came first.

When the ambulance called for him, on this occasion a joy to behold, he was more than ready, clutching his little bag of belongings and dressed in his own clothes that Ma had brought in the previous Sunday. He said goodbye to Paddy and Christy and the nurses at the door and they told him to enjoy himself and that they looked forward to seeing him again. He would certainly comply with the first bit, but would just as certainly do all in his power to deny them the pleasure of the second. A small boy and girl who had arrived in the ambulance stood whimpering and hanging onto their mothers in the hallway. He pitied them and at the same time felt what almost amounted to glee that it wasn't him.

Again he sat up front with the driver and as they drove south his whole being pushed away the city and suburbs, the high red-bricked buildings and mad traffic, impatient for the country and normality. Shortly after passing over Shankill's humpback bridge he could see Bray Head through the trees at Crinken, the cross standing out against the sky. He felt like a right gobdaw when the tears flowed in spite of his best efforts to gulp them back, but he just could not help himself he was so grateful and happy.

'Don't tell me,' the driver said, 'that you're sorry to be gettin' near home.'

Ray blinked at him through the tears and shook his head.

Never had the town of Bray looked as good as it did that day. He gazed out lovingly over everything: the Dargle flowing gently under the bridge; the Royal corner with its customary quota of corner-boys, one of which Ray would grow up to be if Ma's prediction was correct.

The town's two paper-boys, Trowler Murray and his 'apprentice', Chicken Reilly, cried: 'Innerpannery Praise' from their stand at the Dublin Bar. Dad translated it for the boys as 'Independent or Press'. Heart-warming music to his ears.

Further up the street they slowed while Tom Costello herded some cows into his yard, and as they passed the Divil encircled by his stone horse-troughs the Town Hall clock struck midday. More music.

On Killarney Road Mrs.Healy and Maggie Crinnion struggled up Fairy Hill with laden message bags.

When the indicator of the ambulance clicked out and pointed to the right for turning up the Lane he was sure that this was the most wonderful day he would have in his life. Ballywaltrim basked in the May sunshine.

And there was George White, the Lane's farmer, pushing his bike into his gateway and looking around slightly alarmed at seeing an ambulance coming up the Lane. The look changed to a smile of recognition as Ray waved to him. Like Dad, Mr. White smoked a pipe and clenched it between his teeth in the same manner when he smiled.

Din Healy and Mick Jones, both clutching hedge clippers, stood talking at Healy's gate, and Jem Hughes, another dudeen puffer, leaned over his own gate.

He had never really thought about it before he went away, but now he realized he loved all of these familiar faces.

Up the Buildings a group of children stopped their playing on the green to watch the ambulance go around. Bridgie Hughes and the Kavanagh sisters, Kathleen and Marie; Vincent Kirwan and the two Crinnion brothers; Ronnie Turner's sisters Gina and Jacqueline, and Ronnie himself was just coming out of his gate with his bow and arrow at the ready and his black dog, Nicky, at his heels. Ronnie was deadly at making real metal arrowheads.

By the time the ambulance got back down to number fifteen the whole family was out to meet him except Dad, who was at work. They were all a bit shy of him at first. Inside the house the kitchen seemed tiny after the spacious wards and veranda. Ma had made one of her currant cakes on the pan and it was still hot enough to melt the butter as it spread. He lashed into it, answering their questions between gulps and showing them his steels.

He was impatient to get outside, to see everyone and everything at once, and he didn't know where to start. Having stuffed his gut he went out onto the Lane and in no time at all a gang of curious youngsters was trailing after him, staring at his steel-caged leg and asking him how he liked being a cripple. He was dragged into some of the cottages to show the mammies his quare leg.

He felt a bit like old Shit-shit an' Stink, the tramp who came around every now and then with a tattered brown suitcase full of holy pictures which he tried to sell at cottage doors. The kids all followed him along the Lane too, jeering and laughing and looking on him with a nervous mixture of fear and excitement, but keeping a safe distance as he always carried a dangerous-looking walking stick which he swung up into the air at each step, or at any young tormentor who carelessly came within reach.

How the unfortunate soul came to acquire such a colourful moniker was not known but as soon as his squat figure was observed turning into the Lane with his battered old soft hat and raggedy raincoat the cry would go up:

'Here's Shit-shit an' Stink, here's the Mad Lad!'

The Mad Lad was the version used if your Ma was within earshot.

To be fair to the man, Ray had never noticed any unwholesome odours emanating from his person on the occasions he had called to the door and the kids listened goggle-eyed behind Ma's skirt as he explained in his yodelly voice how his present sorry state was the result of his having had the misfortune to be run over by a goods train.

The following days were spent in what was as near to pure contentment as anyone gets on this planet. He roamed around savouring all the old haunts. Sympathetic neighbours handed him the odd penny or ha'penny and he was in and out of Andy's so often that Andy wanted to know did his Mammy win the Fifty or what? His mouth was raw from sucking brown Peggy's Legs and big pink Lucky Lumps. A Lucky Lump was sucked vigorously and with great impatience because there was a chance of being rewarded with the metal taste of a twelve-sided brass English thruppenny bit at its centre.

Ronnie showed him the new wooden soapbox car his dad had made. It was painted bright red and was all ready for

Ronnie to take part in the Bray Soapbox Derby in a few days time at Cuala Road.

Down at the pond he checked to see if any of the minnies he had released into it last summer had survived. The minnies had been carried in jam jars from beneath the Silver Bridge on the Dargle river. Sure enough, there they were making their incredibly quick little darts to and fro in the sunny shallows near the edge of the pond.

In his eagerness to get into Darley's Wood he tore a two-inch gash in his left knee on the barbed wire at the top of Healy's garden. It was nothing. The limbs of most of the youngsters were criss-crossed with the legacies of such minor mishaps.

He ran through the wood, the steels giving him what Dad called a quare gait a' goin', and looked over the high wall at Darley's fierce bull. Even the pig-pong drifting across the wood from the cottage sties was wonderful.

He climbed into Hodson's Wood with the help of a hoosh from one of the lads and skeetered awkwardly down the slides on one leg, over-balancing several times and rolling into the undergrowth. He revelled in the freedom to roll among the bushes and get himself covered in dust and bugs. He hadn't been properly dirty in months. A good shake and he was dragging himself back up the bank by grabbing the laurel branches that hung over the slides.

He wandered by himself up Giltspur Lane beside the wood and climbed into the Ringwood Field by way of the gap behind a large beech tree. This beautiful field swept upwards from the lane towards the slopes of Little Sugarloaf and derived its name from an ancient circle of oaks that surrounded a huge half-buried boulder high up in the field.

Above the treetops the peaks of the mountain nudged their gently rounded humps against the blue. The luxuriant green of new growth was everywhere, and the sweet smell of the sun-warm grass came to him in waves as his happy footsteps brushed their way towards the Ringwood. Halfway up he paused to pat the heads of the field's only occupants, a pair of friendly donkeys.

Seated on the rock in the pleasant shade of the oaks he looked out between their trunks and across the field to the woodlands that almost completely surrounded it. Every tree that he knew of and many that he couldn't put a name to grew here, boughs and leaves mingling in a rich confusion of greens. Here and there a tall pine raised its tip above the undulating canopy of beeches, chestnuts, ashes, birches, oaks hazels and hollies. Lots of hollies.

Hollybrook!

He stayed there for a long time, becoming part of the stillness, letting the peace of this lovely place seep into his bones.

In Butler's field he rolled in the long grass, grinning at the Hairy Mollies, Forty-leggers, Piss-the-mires and God's cows in their world among the roots.

A small shiny snail approached the base of a stem of grass, scouted around it with its antennae, then began to climb up it. The blade was at least eighteen inches high and Ray's grin widened as he foresaw the inevitable. He followed the slow ascent as the snail took a full two minutes to climb ten inches. It was now coming off the round lower stem and onto the flat blade.

With breath held in ecstatic suspense he watched, not risking a blink, while the snail continued upwards until at about the foot mark the blade suddenly buckled and deposited it back on the ground.

Ray chuckled.

Poor Shellacky Boogie.

It had landed on its back so he set it right way up and waited.

Presently there was a tentative poking out of horns and when he was satisfied that the coast was clear Mr. Shellacky made his sluggish way to the same blade of grass and started up again.

Ray laughed out loud and thumped the ground.

Jakers, wasn't that a right gobaloon of a yoke!

Again the grass keeled over and the snail, apparently unfazed by these little setbacks, went at it for the third time.

Oh, poor silly Shellacky Boogie! It's a good feckin' job yer man, Bruce, was lookin' at a spider an' not the likes of you!

He drew great joyful gulps of the richness of the earth into his long-deprived lungs.

Never had there been such a May.

And to cap it all Gina Turner, Ronnie's younger sister, said she would be his girlfriend from now on, cripple or no cripple.

CHAPTER FOURTEEN

Nobody was more surprised than himself at his success in persuading Ma not to send him back to Clontarf. It was seldom indeed that anyone changed Ma's mind, but as his month of idyllic freedom flew by and a new heightened consciousness of the things he loved flooded his soul he spent hours cogitating on arguments to put forward against having the second operation.

Had he known it, of course, he need only have mentioned Nurse Blakely's strange 'turns' and his problem would in all probability have been solved instantly. As it was he stuck to endeavouring to convince her that the left foot didn't look too bad at all now that the right one was done, and that the butchered foot was now encouraging a copycat reaction in the other, and what was the point in wasting the doctor's time?

And he prayed.

Hail Marys one after the other until the words got all mixed up. He Hail Maryed himself to sleep every night and woke up Hail Marying in the morning, and to his amazement and delight it worked. He thought he was hearing things when Ma said sure maybe we'll chance it and trust in God that it'll be all right.

He reeled off another string of Hail Marys in thanksgiving and vowed never to be a little get again as long as he lived.

One day later in the summer Michael O'Connell, the boy from Drumcondra whose bed had been opposite Ray's in the hospital ward, arrived at Ballywaltrim with his father in their car. They drove Ray to Dublin Airport where they spent the afternoon watching from the roof as the Fokker Friendships and shiny new Aer Lingus Viscounts took off and landed. They had tea at the O'Connell home in Homefarm Park. Michael's parents were very nice and his Ma spread the table with lovely cakes, the kind you bought in shops, and there were carpets on all the floors. Ma would be in her alley in a house like this.

Michael had a marvellous train set laid out on the floor in the front room. An electric train! Jakers, was there no end to the things you could have if you were rich? The only other electric train Ray had ever seen was going round and round in a shop window the time Aunt Kitty had brought him to Dublin for Christmas.

Darkness was falling as they started back for Bray. Dad was to have met them at the Divil but they arrived a little earlier than the arranged time and drove slowly on, watching for him in the beams of the car's headlights as they pierced the gloom of Killarney Road.

'There he is! That's me Daddy.'

They spotted him at the top of Fairy Hill, pedalling hard and puffing on the pipe, his bicycle lamp swinging from side to side with each push on the pedals. He jumped off, running a few steps with the bike, as Mr. O'Connell sounded the horn.

Having said their goodbyes and thanked the O'Connells, they stood and watched as the car reversed into the gateway of a big house called Ripley and turned back for Dublin. When the tail lights had vanished into the night father and son turned and walked down the other side of the hill, Dad winking the lamp on and off every so often to light their way while Ray told him about his day out.

121

As they neared home and the bottom light welcomed them through the branches of the Big Tree, Ray knew in his heart of hearts that he wouldn't swap Ballywaltrim for all the electric trains in Toyland.

Twice a week he had to attend the outpatients department of the hospital for physiotherapy, travelling to and from Merrion Street on the 45 bus. The free travel vouchers supplied by Mr. Brophy the welfare officer didn't cover Ma so he had to get used to the idea of travelling alone.

He hated it, and the journey on the bus always made him feel nauseous. He usually sat opposite the open door watching the kerb racing past, veering in and out like a gramophone needle when it reaches the end of a record, and listening to the changes in the roar of the wheels as the bus sped past walls, gateways, hedges and open spaces.

As autumn approached the trips to Dublin came to a welcome end when he was told he could attend a physiotherapist in a little room over Vance and Wilson's chemist shop in Bray, and the visits were cut down to one a week.

Ronnie woke him one morning at six o'clock by knocking on his bedroom window and the pair of them went off up to the Ringwood Field to gather mushrooms. They each plucked a long stem of grass to thread their harvest onto for carrying home. As it happened that morning the harvest was a meagre one, but their early rising was made worthwhile by the pleasure of seeing the big sloping field in the morning sunlight, its beauty increased by the magic of a scintillating veil of dew.

He still wore his steels and although they were now loose and threatening to fall apart he managed to make them last until he went back to school in September. Those steels maintained his celebrity status and he was determined to hold onto them until they disintegrated beyond repair.

'Well, well! Fáilte ar ais, stráinséir!' Mr. Donegan exclaimed as Ray entered the classroom flaunting a limp that was noticeably more pronounced than it had been of late.

Welcome back, stranger!

And to fourth class at that. Although he had been absent for the greater part of third class and had done no exams Mr. Donegan had decided he should go straight on to fourth, and he quaked at the prospect of having to catch up on all he had missed and maybe being looked upon as the class dunce until he had done so. Another great thing about being a cripple was you didn't have to worry about school bullies. The big lads from Wolfe Tone Square wouldn't be out to split you while you had a gammy leg.

Wolfe Tone Square was built about ten years before the cottages at Ballywaltrim, and so was home to a large population of older kids. The Square could be used as a short cut to or from school but was seldom taken advantage of because no Ballywaltrimer was prepared to risk a batin' at the hands of the Wolfe Toners. Should a youngster happen to trip and fall on his way from school and arrive home plastered in a mixture of mud and blood, the worried mammy was likely to ask had 'yeh come through Wolfe Tone or what?'

Ray and Val were often in the Square, usually on a Sunday with Dad visiting his sisters, Aunts Sarah and Moira. Aunt Sarah threw wonderful birthday parties and hooleys with fiddle and accordion players, the kids warned to wait upstairs until called down to find the table spread with a sumptuous display of goodies.

Any time Dad visited one of his sisters he had to call on the other as well or they would fall out with each other and with him and might not be on speaking terms for months.

Such bloody rot!' Ma would say. 'Typical whingin' Cranleys for your life!' Dad had lived in the Square himself for a few years, having moved up from St. Kevin's Square when Wolfe Tone was built, the first major housing estate outside the town.

It was on the occasion of Granda Cranley's funeral, the first one Ray had ever attended, that he first heard Ma refer to the whingin' Cranleys'. One of Dad's sisters was rather loud in bewailing her sad loss and afterwards Ma had remarked:

'Did yeh hear yer one scutterin' out of her in the graveyard? "Ah, me poor Daddy, me poor Daddy." A bit late now to start worryin' about her poor Daddy when the man's goin' into the clay. Answer her better to have looked after him while he was above ground. But no, didn't give a shite about him while he was in it, an' now whingin' just for oul' goster when it's as much use to him as a shaggin' alarm clock.'

Granda was seventy-nine, which made him seventy-two years older than Ray's classmate Bernard Egan whose funeral he had attended around the same time. He had played a game of taws with the redheaded little Bernard in the schoolyard the day before he died in a fall from the Cliff Walk at Bray Head. The whole class had walked from school to the Holy Redeemer church for his funeral Mass. It had taken a long time for the finality of it to sink in.

That dead was dead.

Bullies, along with all other wrongdoers, must be forgiven if what Mr. Donegan preached was to be heeded. Loving thy neighbour, he would explain, didn't only refer to the people on your own road. It meant loving all mankind including your worst enemy.

'It even means,' he would pronounce gravely, 'that we must love and forgive the English. Yes! The pagan English. The same mortal enemy that enslaved our beloved land for centuries. God's ways may appear strange to us, but we must not question his word.'

The only English person Ray was acquainted with was old Mrs. Valentine next door and she was a likeable old soul who had no Irish slaves that he knew of.

Mr. Donegan also had strong feelings about youngsters playing soccer.

'An uncivilised game, running around throwing their heads at the ball. No wonder they are all half mad.'

Ray wasn't particularly interested in football one way or the other, but he reckoned he would rather head a football than have his skull on the receiving end of a lick of a hurley stick.

When word reached Ballywaltrim that a grotto was being erected in the middle of Wolfe Tone Square with a statue of the Blessed Virgin in it everyone was much relieved. There had obviously been a dramatic change of heart in the Square if they were engaged in such a pious project. Ma said the Blessed Virgin would protect anyone passing through anyway.

Before she and Dad married Ma had worked for one of the Quality, a Mrs. Browne who lived in a big house called Milverton on the Burnaby Estate in Greystones, and Ma continued to visit there now and again for some years afterwards. Threats of terrible vengeance in the event of them making a show of her in front of Mrs. Browne were issued to the boys on setting out. Before ringing the doorbell she would check that the pair of them were spotless.

'C'mere till I wipe your clock,' she would say, spitting on her hankie and rubbing their faces until it felt like the bones were showing, while they squirmed and held their breaths.

'Good afternoon, moddom.'

She sounded like her mouth was full of bottlers. Moddom would lead them through the house to the red-tiled kitchen where she and Ma would have a cup of tea. The boys were banished to the back lawn to extract what entertainment they could from Raider the dog.

'And how are Mawster Alan and Mistress Felicia?' Ma enquired after the Browne children, her swanky accent working overtime. It was probably here that she picked it up in the first place. At home she said 'maybe', but in Browne's it was all 'p'raps' this and 'p'raps' that. She said Mr. Browne was a big knob in Guinness's Brewery and that someday he might get the lads into the coopers' shed, whatever the flames that was.

As they left the Burnaby Ma would point out an eating establishment on the main road where she had been a waitress at an even earlier period. Now called The Copper Kettle, in Ma's time it had gone under the title of The Bonne Bouche, a name that inspired inexplicable hilarity in the children whenever she mentioned it.

'Bomboosh!' they would howl, rolling around the place. The picture in Ray's mind was of a cannonball dropping into a lake.

In complete contrast to Milverton was the little whitewashed Coolagad Cottage, high on a hill between the Glen o' the Downs and Windgates, where some relations called Cullen lived. Getting off the 84 at the head of Windgates they would walk down the back road along by Belmont Wood until they came to the stone stile that took them over the high wall into the Belmont Estate. Ma knew her way everywhere. They crossed the fields passing the lonely ruins of an old mansion, and nearby the gaping door of an underground ice-house.

In early summer primroses by the thousand bloomed on the grassy banks here, and carpeted the level area bordering the pond. Like Darley's pond, the air above it was alive with a myriad whizzing insects.

The big wooden gate that led onto the road at Upper Templecarrig posed no problem for Ma. She would hoosh both of them safely over and then scale it herself with all the agility of a Sugarloaf goat.

Cullen's cottage was quaint and very dark inside, the windows being tiny, but once your eyes got used to the gloom it was lovely to watch the shafts of sunlight sloping in through the open door and windows, just like the beams that came down from the sky in the holy pictures. The cottage had been built in the nineteenth century by an ancestor of the present occupants who had been employed as butcher to the local landlords, the La Touche family.

The roof, originally of thatch, was now corrugated iron, and most of the furniture had been made by another long-departed Cullen. Old Sis Cullen was the object of Ma's visits. She lived there with her sister Mary and brother John. They grew a few apple trees, which Dad pruned for them when necessary, and on an autumn visit Sis would send them home laden with fruit.

The sisters were unmarried and, typical of the older folk of their day, dressed in a dreary combination of black and grey. But Sis was by no means grey in personality; she had a turn of phrase that kept the kids in kinks and Ma wincing.

The road up to Coolagad Cottage from the back gate of Belmont was narrow and winding, and the weary-legged boys would pester Ma with cries of: 'Is that it?' each time a chimney appeared above the hedge-rows ahead of them, until finally they arrived at Cullen's to be welcomed by Sis's cheerful if somewhat impolite greeting:

'Come in! Come in, the whole lot of yiz, an' if yeh can't find a chair yeh can stick yer thumb up yer arse an' sit on yer elbow!'

With bony fingers she would hold the lads at arms length.

'I declare to me paint, yiz's growin' up so fast I can't tell the other from which! Don't forget what I told yeh now, Lulu, if the next one's a little filly, call her after poor oul' Sis.'

She told them about her older brother, Nick, now 'outa print an' below ground with them gone before', who in earlier times owned a sidecar that he hired as a hackney. Nick did not take kindly to the coming of the motor car and whenever one passed him and his horse on the road he would lash out at it with his whip, the 'eyes rowlin' in his head with rage' and a stream of venomous curses raining down on the puzzled motorist.

In autumn most of the boys in the cottages got their new 'Brophy Boots', so called because they were obtained by means of vouchers supplied by the welfare officer of that name. Tough, heavy boots they were, with steel 'horseshoes' on the heels that produced showers of bright sparks if a lad kicked them against the ground as he ran along the Lane on dusky evenings.

The change to Brophy Boots from light sandals or canvas runners resulted in skinned heels and ankles until young feet became accustomed to the hard leather. All shoe repairs were carried out at home by Dad himself, the smell of freshly cut leather filling the house as he shaped soles and heels from a new sheet, and bent over the cobbler's last tapping in metal 'Segs' to prolong the life of the repair.

Back to school meant that now and again the kids came home with their heads walking, and the method of ridding the hair of these hoppers was not a pleasant one. Ma would dip a rag in paraffin oil and rub it into their hair, then proceed to scrape their skulls with a fine-tooth comb until the tears streamed down their cheeks. Now and then there would be a pause in the scraping while she dispatched a louse between her thumbnails with a sharp little crack

The whiff of paraffin hung about their heads for days, defying all attempts at washing it away and making them feel like walking rush-lights.

CHAPTER FIFTEEN

'Find that shaggin' pliers, or as sure as Jaysus swung on the cross I'll pulverize the whole whorin' lot of yiz.'

Ma didn't like to curse.

'I hate it as I hate the Devil,' she would say, and when she purged her soul in the confessional not as much as a feck would be heard out of her until the next temper got her. Then, as soon as she let a single expletive slip from her lips, the dam would burst and a withering torrent would pour forth unhindered and terrible. She could plumb incredible depths with a 'string of French ones' as Mrs. Jones called them.

When the kids came in from school she had been in exceptionally good humour, regaling them with stories of her own schooldays, even managing to make light of how she used to hide under the bed when her father arrived home drunk, and how he would use the sweeping brush to beat her in her hiding place.

And she told of her grandfather, Tom 'The Horn' Byrne, who had lived at Templecarrig Lodge in the previous century and claimed to be descended from the same family as the 1798 rebel, Billy Byrne of Ballymanus. He would boast of this connection when tanked up with porter and looking for a row.

'Oh now, he was a quare customer, an' if he was fed up with somebody pratin' out of them he'd say "I'd sooner listen to an oul' goat pissin' on a bodhran". '

And then the stupid chickens escaped from the hen-run

130

They lost no time in getting down to the serious business of scratching craters in the flowerbeds. Still in good form, Ma whooped as she chased after and caught them one by one and lifted them flapping and fluttering over the top of the wire netting.

'The divil skewer them anyway, gettin' out like that,' she said, inspecting the hole through which they had made their short-lived bid for freedom. 'I better get the pliers an' fix it before they're out again on me.'

She pulled the wire together temporarily and vanished into the shed for about five minutes, after which time she emerged plierless.

'Did any of yiz see the pliers?'

A negative shaking of young heads.

'Isn't that the divil's flint now. Where the flames can it have got to?'

She went in to search the house.

Sensing that the situation could quite easily escalate to temper level if not defused without delay, the kids joined in the search, probing every hole and corner for the missing tool without success.

It still hadn't been located when Dad dismounted at the gate and wheeled his bike up the path, no doubt hoping for a nice quiet evening after a hard days slogging at the convent.

'Ah, thanks bitta God,' he sighed, plonking himself down at the table. 'An' how are yiz all, what?'

'How are we indeed,' Ma snapped and stalked off into the girls' room from whence presently came sailing shoes, clothes, comics and miscellaneous other items accompanied by muttered complaints about lazy bitches' ghosts who wouldn't do a hands turn for a body. They all knew that when Ma took to tidying out a room it was very often the prelude to a temper, but as she had been to confession on Saturday and it was now only Monday, they were hopeful that she might not start cursing.

Dad finished his tea in the midst of constant bombardment from the room, then moved over into their ancient and only armchair by the range. He lit his pipe and sat back. In the room the sweeping brush slammed and banged against the skirting board with increasing ferocity as Ma voiced detailed descriptions of the family's deficiencies. Then she was standing in the doorway, lips pursed making her mouth resemble the cutting edge of a Mac's Smile razorblade.

'Hey, you!' she addressed Dad as though she had never laid eyes on him before.

'Me?' he asked between puffs.

'Yes, fool, you. Who the shaggin' hell else would I be talkin' to? Where's the pliers?'

'It should be in the shed,' he offered helpfully.

'It should be in the shed. It should be in the shed.' she mimicked him. 'Of course it should be in the fuckin' shed, but amn't I after scourin' house an' shed from top to bottom an' not a curse-a-God sign of it. So don't sit there on your arse all night. Get up an' find it.'

'Will yeh for God's sake give us a bitta peace,' he pleaded,' I'm wore out.'

'You're worn out! An' what afuckingbout me? Slaving here for you an' your rotten kids day in an' day out an' no thanks for it only what misery yiz can make for me. An' now yiz've gone an' made me curse an' me only after bein' to Confession. Jaysus Christ forgive every one of yiz, yiz whore's melts, yiz fuckers. I'm sorry I ever had kids. Sorry to the heart's core I am'

'But Mammy,' a small voice asked, 'if yeh didn't want us, why did yeh born us?'

There was no break in the flow of invective.

'I was a lovely woman before I had yous. A lovely woman. A woman who never used a bad word. Wouldn't even say "bloody", an' now look at me! Yiz have me eternal soul damned. But then, a-course, Jaysus knows they were never chastised properly. If that was a proper father sittin' in the chair there...'

She made a sudden swipe at Dad's feet with the brush, missing her target as Dad lifted his legs and the head of the brush struck the fender with an unmelodious clang.

Dad, as tired and tormented as he was, could not suppress a mischievous chuckle. Such was the man's sense of humour. Ma, not surprisingly, saw no reason for merriment.

'Yes, that's it. Go on, laugh! It's all yer bastardinwell good for. Yer useless just like yer oul' fella before yeh. Useless! Useless! Useless!'

Ray knew that the tears welling up in his Dad's eyes were drawn there as much by her remarks about his father as by those directed at himself. He had seen it before. Dad must have really loved Granda.

The children sat about, cowering in silence and trying to be invisible, fearful of the moment Ma might turn her wrath on them. Dad glanced over at them and winked, squeezing out a tear that hesitated for a second before streaking on down his cheek. Ray wanted to run and throw his arms around him but didn't dare move. With the tip of his tongue he licked his own tears.

Dad took his pipe from his mouth.

'Now you lave that man alone, an' he dead an' gone.'

'Ay, he's dead an' gone now all right, but he drove your mother into an early grave before him. All he was good for was sittin' in the corner with the dudeen stuck in his gob while she took everything on her shoulders. A fuckin' oul' gobshite, an' you're the very same.'

'Lave him alone, yeh bad oul' rip,' he said in what was as near as he ever came to a shout, adding quietly; 'An' don't be upsettin' the poor kids.'

'Oh, sweet Jaysus!' she beseeched the Sacred Heart in her Holy Communion picture above the mantelpiece. 'Will yeh listen to that man talkin' through his arse. The kids. The poor bloody kids. If yeh had upset them a bit more long ago they wouldn't be such little shites today.'

'Ah, now...'

'Shut up! Sure you're not a man at all. Any real man would cut the arse off a child who didn't obey.'

'Ay, maybe so,' Dad ventured, 'but he might kick the arse off the likes a' you as well.'

The air crackled for a second or two before Ma launched into a shrieking tirade. 'I'm fuckin' tellin' yiz. I'm warnin' every bastardin' one of yiz. I'm master and mistress in this house and my word is law, an' as true as Jaysus if yiz don't do as I say in future I'll strike that final blow. Yes, the final blow will be struck. Do yiz hear me? Yiz devils unhung, yiz rotten whore's melts. Answer me!'

She kicked at a few random ankles.

Hoarsely whispered yeses from the kids.

'An' you?' She thumped Dad's shoulder causing his pipe to fall into his lap, whereupon he leapt to his feet to shake off the hot ash, and in doing so struck his head off the partly open door of the kitchen press. The old clock jangled madly.

'Now look what yeh made me do with yer oul' carry on,' he complained, rubbing his head vigorously.

'An' you?' she insisted with another thump.

'Ah, what ails yeh, for God's sake?'

'Are yeh goin' to do exactly as I say from this night on?'

'Yis...yis. Now lave me alone for the luvva God.'

Bedtime couldn't come quickly enough. Bed meant a respite, however temporary, from the battlefield. Blankets pulled tightly over the head would muffle the sounds of conflict while prayers were earnestly hurled out across the universe to God or anyone else who might happen to be listening to intervene and stop the ructions.

Only when Ma and Dad had gone to bed and all was quiet did Ray allow his eyes to wearily close. He was always in dread of something terrible happening if he slept during a temper. Suppose Ma decided to strike the final blow? At least

135

he would have a chance to run for help as soon as the first blood-curdling scream rent the air, assuming, of course, that she started her rounds with one of the others.

Asleep he could wind up with his skull split open, and the rest of the family the same. Ma always said the hatchet was the right weapon for the job.

For many months that missing pliers featured prominently in Ma's tempers. No matter what she happened to be giving out about she would finish with: 'And find that pliers!'

And find it they eventually did, long after Ma had passed away. It was exactly where everyone thought it should have been. In the shed. Only it had fallen from its shelf to lie hidden between the sheets of galvanised iron of which the old shed was constructed.

CHAPTER SIXTEEN

Ma was out of sight in the front room. Ray heaped more and more sugar onto his bowl of porridge until it resembled a well-iced Christmas cake. He liked lashings of sugar. When his porridge bowl was nearly empty he observed that the sugar bowl was in a similar state. Ma would be bound to notice. He tiptoed over to the kitchen press and gingerly opened the creaky door. It smelled lovely in there, made you want to stick your head in and leave it there all day. He took out the blue sugar bag and topped the bowl up to the level he thought it should be at.

He was closing the door again when Ma came in the cross door.

'What are yeh lookin' for in there?'

'Nothin' he answered truthfully.

'Well, finish yer porridge there an' go down for the milk. Ask Mrs. White if she can spare an extra pint this mornin'. We're usin' twice as much with yiz all off school.'

He grabbed the milk can and went out. It was only half past nine and already the sun was hot. The Lane still had the sleepy stillness of morning about it, but soon the first of the youngsters would appear from the cottages kicking at stones until they found something better to do, or yodelling at the gates for their friends. It was no longer a dusty lane. The County Council had recently surfaced it with stones of a warm amber colour, and kids had trailed behind the steamroller chanting the word it seemed to say as it chuffed along:

'Cath-ec-ism! Cath-ec-ism! Cath-ec-ism!'

The country was in the middle of a glorious and seemingly never-ending heat wave. White's back door was open and the gorgeous aroma of frying rashers drifted out into the yard as he approached. He could hear them sizzling on the pan when Mrs. White appeared in answer to his knock.

'Well, Raymond?' She was chewing on a piece of rasher.

'Mammy wants to know can she have an extra pint today please.'

'We'll soon see.'

She walked across to the tiny dairy opposite the back door, where the cool milky-smelling shade was refreshing and pleasant.

'Ah, yes, sure there's plenty.'

She stood her pint measure on the floor and tilted the big milk churn to fill it. Milk didn't pour tinkling like water; it creamed and curled into the measure, soft-bubbling and gurgling in its richness. Three times she filled the measure, then poured in a generous tilly, leaving Ray's can more than three-quarters full.

'There yeh go now, young Cranley. Don't spill any of that goin' up the Lane.'

'I won't. Thanks, Missus White.'

It was not a needless caution. A little while back he had spilled the whole can over himself and the lane while attempting to do a 'windmill', swinging the can up and over in circles, depending on centrifugal force to hold the precious contents in place. He still winced at the memory. Oul' Jem

Hughes breakin' his shite laughin' at him. No use trying to tell Ma he had tripped over something. The whole Lane would soon know. Ma had sent him red-faced back down to White's to explain the calamity and cadge some more milk.

Mrs. White had said wasn't he the right little cur.

He used to think she was called Mrs. White because she sold milk.

Spilled milk was nothing new to the Lane. During the milk strike of 1953 it had run white with deliberately spilled churns. Mrs. White, not wishing to let her neighbours down, managed for a while to let them have their usual quota by having them pass their cans over the fences of the back gardens in a sort of milk chain. Word of this neighbourly arrangement got out somehow and one evening Dad came in saying that 'a gang of lousers was throwin' poor oul' White's milk out.'

Ray sprinted down to join the excited crowd already assembled at the scene. Three angry-looking individuals stood watching the broad white stream as it flowed down the slope onto the main road.

'That'll fuckin' learn them!' the biggest said, slapping his hands together and getting into a car parked in the centre of the entrance to the lane. The other two followed and they drove off in the direction of Hollybrook.

This morning with his full can Ray picked his way down White's stony drive.

'Good Noel!' he shouted across to Noel Healy who was leaning against the Big Tree as he emerged from White's gate. Noel was crunching on a big green apple.

'Good Raymond!'

139

'Where did yeh get the apple?'

'Butler's orchard.'

'Giz the buttsie.'

'OK.' Noel examined the apple core, took one last bite out of it and lobbed it across the Lane to Ray. He caught it without splashing a drop of milk on the ground.

'Thanks. See yeh, Noel.'

There was a fair amount of apple left on the buttsie. Ray always left a decent bit when giving his buttsie to somebody and Noel was the same, but some lads would hand it to you with the pips hanging out.

Before reaching his own gate, and while still hidden from view of his house by Valentine's hedge, he lifted the can to his lips and took a long satisfying swig of the still-warm milk. He decided that he would spend the tuppence he had in his pocket on a can of buttermilk from Dan Buckley at Switzer's of Ballywaltrim Grove.

'She didn't give much of a tilly,' Ma remarked as she transferred the milk into jugs and handed the can back to him.

Oh feck, found out again.

He slunk guiltily out the back door with the can and as he passed the kitchen window Ma stuck her head out.

'Keep me a drop of the buttermilk an' I'll do a currant cake on the pan for tea.'

'Great! Yeah, righto, I'll keep yeh some.'

Currant cake! And it's not even Sunday!

Andy was opening his shop as he came by and he was tempted for a second to spend half his money on one of Andy's ice lollies. Andy made them in eggcups and had to twist them this way and that to free them for customers. You could suck all of the colour out and be left with a block of ice.

'Hello there! That has the makin's of a real paint-peeler,' Andy said, shielding his eyes with his arm as he gazed into the morning blue. 'Are yeh buyin'?'

Wouldn't be enough buttermilk left for Ma if he only got a penny's worth.

'No, goin' for buttermilk.'

'Oh, no better man for this class of a day. Atin' an' drinkin' in it. Good luck, so.'

At the brow of the hill he stood at the corner of Ballywaltrim Lane and waited while a car laboured up out of the Hollybrook dip, and, sputtering with relief, rolled on towards Bray.

He crossed the road to the entrance of Switzer's. Dan Buckley and his wife lived in the gate lodge with its bright red windows and doors, but the dairy was in the basement of the big house. Inside the gate Ray turned to his right, leaving the main avenue and taking the shady path through the trees, a short cut to the dairy.

Mrs. Buckley filled the can and gave him a small block of freshly made butter for Ma and asked how was everyone below. He said they were all grand.

Coming back beneath the trees he drank his fill of the sweet-sour buttermilk, swallowing with relish the golden butter-nuggets that floated on top. His eyes squinted against the radiant greenness of millions of beech leaves as he drank, his head tilted back. Here and there the sunlight broke through the canopy in dazzling diamond swords that transformed the dust that rose around his feet into countless specks of light.

There hadn't been a drop of rain for weeks and he noticed that the old roadside well near Switzer's gate had dried up. He conjured up the ghosts of ancient Ballywaltrim folk who would have come there to fill their jugs and buckets, and swap the gossip of their day. Further down the road he stopped to lean on the wooden gate opposite Lawlor's lodge.

Shaded by a crab-apple tree, the fruit of which Mrs. Lawlor said would 'kill yeh down dead with stummick ache,' he looked away off to Little Sugarloaf and the Faraway Trees. Some of the older boys had been to the top of the mountain hunting for rabbits with their dogs, and they said you could see Kilmacanogue from up there. That village was only a few miles south of Ballywaltrim but Ray had never been there. He longed to join the Faraway Trees in their trek across the hills.

A few of the lads from the cottages shouted to him as they passed by, darting here and there after an old tennis ball they were kicking along the middle of the road.

'Are yeh comin' up to Hudson's for a go on the slides?'

He shook his head.

'OK, well folly us up later if yeh change yer mind.'

In the lane girls chanted skipping rhymes as the long rope turned by Ann and Ita Healy slapped against the ground throwing little clouds into the air, while a line of impatient young-ones waited their turn to jump in, do their bit, and jump out again without tripping on the rope and making a hames of it.

'All in together girls

This fine weather girls

The cows in the meadow

Moo moo...'

He left the can with Ma's share of the buttermilk on the floor inside the front door alongside the milk jug and a saucer that contained four sausages. He pushed the sausages to one side, making room for the bit of butter. The draught coming under the door was a blessing in summer but they had to throw old coats down to stop the east wind in winter.

The exciting idea of having a go at climbing Little Sugarloaf danced around in his head. Sure what could go wrong? He couldn't get lost anyway; any loolah knew which way was down.

By the time Dad came in for his dinner 'parched with the droot an' drenched with parspiration' Ray had made his mind up to attempt the conquest of the mountain. They tucked into their spuds and mushy peas to the accompaniment of familiar commercials for Urney's Chocolates and Donnelly's Sausages, and each fifteen minute segment of Radio Eireann's sponsored programmes seemed to take an hour today.

'Go outside there, one of yiz, an' listen for the quarter,' Dad requested.

Ray went out and threw himself on the small back lawn which Dad had recently cut slowly and laboriously with the hedge clippers. The lawn at the front was much bigger and could take the best part of two days to clip, with everyone taking turns at clipping, their knees stained bright green as they inched across the grass. Joneses in number eleven had a hand pushed lawnmower and Ray thought for a long time that Ma was referring to this family when she gave out about people trying to keep up with the Joneses.

The 'quarter' was the sounding of the hooter at the Dargle and Bray Laundry at a quarter to two, and Dad always left for the convent at its call as if for some odd reason he trusted neither clock nor wireless to oblige him with the correct time. Another reliable reminder of the time of day was Darley's garden bell whose tolling was heard across the fields at five minutes to two, calling the local farmhands and gardeners back to their toil.

Ray accompanied Dad as far as the gate and told him of his plan for the afternoon.

'For God's sake be careful, son. I've never gone up from this side meself. Would yeh not wait till some other day an' maybe we could go up together?'

'Ah Dad, I'll be all right, honest. I'll turn back if it looks too risky.'

'Did yeh tell yer Mammy?'

'Not yet.'

'Well, make sure yeh do then, an' water the celery before yeh go. I'll see yiz all at teatime, please God. Bye now.'

He scooted a bit, then pedalled down the Lane and out of sight. Old Mr. Valentine came out of his gate next door and shouted a big rusty 'Hello there' as he threw his enormous size twelve boot over his ancient bike and followed Dad down the hill. He would be heading for the picturesque Kilbride Church where he had been verger since the early years of the century.

The whole back garden was planted with rows of celery, Dad having rented it to a man called Dawson for the season for four pounds. It had to be watered every day and Ma would fill the big green enamel jug and the milk can from the tap inside the kitchen window, handing them out over the windowsill to the boys. It seemed to take forever to get it all watered until they got smart and realized that you got around a lot quicker if you weren't over-generous with the water. All things in moderation, as Ma was fond of saying.

'I'm goin' up the fields,' he told Ma in a pared down version of the truth.

No sense chancing her putting the kybosh on his adventure. He crossed what they called the Football Field although the only goalposts it ever boasted were piles of gansies and jackets, and jumped over the gully with its trickle of a stream that separated it from the next field. At the top corner of the fourth field stood the remains of an old mud cabin known locally as the Clay House.

Brambles were the only occupants now and they grew unhindered through gaps in the walls that had once been door and windows. The sad little ruin was slowly returning to the earth.

As he approached it he almost tripped over Jem Redmond who lived at number nine with his elderly sister, Mrs. Dawson. Jem was lying asleep in the long grass, his soft hat covering his eyes and his dog, Shep, at his side. Shep jumped up and ran to Ray, yelping excitedly, and Jem lifted his hat.

145

'Who...? Ah, the hard! An' where might you be off to, tell me?'

'I'm goin' to climb Sugarloaf, Mister Redmond,' he announced proudly.

'Ho begod, better you than me then. This is far enough for Jem. It's the breathin', don't yeh know. Me oul' bellows is bollixed.'

He gave a wheezy cough as if to demonstrate.

'I was havin' a grand snooze till that yoke there started yowlin' out of him,' he said, throwing his hat at Shep who grabbed it between his jaws and brought it back to him.

He lay back with a contented sigh and replaced the hat over his face.

'Good luck to yeh, me lad,' he waved a hand. 'Give us a shout if I'm still here on your way down. Don't wanta miss the bit t'ate.'

'Righto.'

Ray climbed through the gap beside the ruin and into the field below Giltspur, Lodge. An old couple called Connolly lived there, and from the kitchen window at home it looked tiny. Seeing it up close was like looking at a picture that has been taken down after hanging for years high on a wall. Halfway up the field was a small pool used by cattle as a drinking place. Water trickled into it from a narrow iron pipe and it teemed with tadpoles. Too bad he hadn't got a jam jar to catch some. He lay on the grassy mound above the pipe and lowered his face until the cold water filled his mouth, then swallowed.

Crossing the lane near the lodge he entered the Ringwood Field and headed for the path through the strip of woodland where he and Dad had gathered sticks on a very different kind of day.

From here on he was in unknown territory. A few fields higher up he discovered hidden in the woods a tower with a granite plaque bearing the inscription G.H. 1849 over the doorway. He guessed the H was for Hodson. Venturing in through the door-less opening he looked up and saw, just beyond his reach, the remains of a wooden spiral staircase leading up to a clear blue circle of sky. It was cool inside the tower and a little scary to hear the faint ghostly whistling of the air in the flue-like structure. Before moving on he scratched his name on the inside wall with a sharp stone.

Making his way ever higher through the fields he stopped every now and then to look back, his heart thumping with a wild joy and a wonderful sense of freedom pervading his whole being.

Fields, ditches, mountains and trees reeled in kaleidoscopic confusion as he ran madly, stumbling, tumbling and rolling in the lush meadow-grass, his laughter not far short of hysterical.

Following a trail through some more woodland he presently came to a large iron gate in a high stone wall. The gate was locked so he scaled the wall to the right of it and found himself on the furze-covered open slopes of Little Sugarloaf.

Countless tiny needles perforated his bare legs as he pushed his way through the densely growing bushes, making him wish he were fourteen and in longers. In places the furze was so high and the path so narrow he had to hold his hands above his head.

Over to his left a dry-stone wall climbed along with him and stretched far ahead up and over the eastern side of the peaks before vanishing down behind the mountain. He made for the wall and came to a grassy patch where a broken gateway had once been the entrance to a stone cottage on the other side. The tumbling walls of the house baked in the heat. He scouted around hoping to find a spring to slake his thirst after the climb but had no success. Sitting to rest on a windowsill he wondered who could have lived in such a lonely beautiful place.

Where did they get their water? And what had happened to them that they deserted the homestead? Oddly, while the cottage itself was crumbling, the pigsty beside it was in perfect order. Great Aunt Lizzie in Windgates used to keep a pig and called him 'the gentleman who pays the rent.'

God, he was thirsty!

All was still except for the chittering of an unseen bird and as he sat daydreaming on the warm stone of the windowsill he found himself starting to nod off.

Ah, here, feck this for a game a' cowboys.

He stood up and shook himself.

Just above the cottage a line of old pine trees grew along the eastern side of the wall and extended to the base of the first rocky peak. He lazily climbed another few hundred yards, and, on that glorious summer's day in 1955, stood among the Faraway Trees.

He ran the palms of his hands over the rough bark of their tall trunks, touching in wonder friends he had observed from afar for so long. His eyes gazed out over the heart-staggering beauty of the valley, his valley, spread out below him; a vast patchwork of woods, fields and mountains sweeping right down to the town of Bray beside the sea. He scanned the landscape and picked out the tiny white curve that was the Lane, a trinket set in endless acres of emerald.

A black insect-like spot moved slowly up the Lane, and as far as he could make out seemed to be pushing a bicycle.

Din Healy? Paddy Messitt?

It was too early for Dad.

Straining to see, he managed to discern the dot in the white gable of number fifteen; the kitchen window from where he had so often mused upon the Faraway Trees, and now here he was at the edge of the unknown looking back over the green valley that had been his whole world until today.

A strange and wonderful ecstasy welled up in him as he surveyed the scene. Far across the valley the copper-green spire of Enniskerry church stood out from the darker green of the surrounding trees. Closer he could see the roof of Hollybrook House and nearby the bright red tiles of Ballywaltrim Grove. The new glass factory on Boghall Road sat like a little white box in the fields. It looked out of place, as indeed it was, it being unusual to see a factory so far out in the country.

Not far from the factory a line of rooftops denoted Boghall Cottages. One of these was used as the local dispensary and Ma went there every Thursday to get the cod liver oil and any medical supplies the family might require.

She had been upset and not a little puzzled one morning when not one of the patients in the waiting room spoke to her or even nodded in response to her observations on the state of the weather. She learned later that the reason behind this sudden bewildering dispensing of cold shoulder was her headscarf. It had been sent to her as a gift by Uncle Jack and Aunt Chris in England, and was a souvenir of Queen Elizabeth's coronation, colourful scenes from that event adorning every inch of it.

'Well, for Christ sake did yeh ever hear such a load of oul' tripe? Not that I give a God's curse about any a' them, sittin' around down there every week discussin' texture a' their last shite.'

And Wolfe Tone, from up here it was indeed a square!

The spire of Christ Church and the tower of the Holy Redeemer rose above the rooftops of Bray, and beyond the graceful curve of Killiney Bay, Dalkey Island shimmered in the distance.

He left the Faraway Trees behind and was scrambling up the first peak when he heard noises on the rocks ahead. Looking up, he found himself confronted with a herd of about a dozen wild goats led by a fierce-looking Billy with huge curling horns. His first instinct was to run screaming for Ma, but as the goats didn't appear to be making any moves towards him he stood his ground and watched them. They stared back at him, motionless as statues.

Mother a' God, those horns look deadly dangerous.

The wall was about fifty yards to his left and he moved carefully in that direction. Twelve goats' heads turned in unison as twenty-four goat's eyes followed his progress towards what he hoped would be safety. When he got near enough he made a dash and in seconds was looking back at them from the other side.

He saw with great relief that they had made no attempt to follow him and most of them were now clambering about the rocks unconcernedly, although the big Billy was still gazing in the direction of the wall. Ray made his way up along the far side until he had put a decent distance between himself and the herd, then climbed back to the western side, dismissing the thought that they might spread out and trap him on the way down.

He trotted along the stony track that linked the peaks singing 'Sippin' Soda' and thinking what a strange name for a girl and wondering why the man was looking at her through a straw.

At the top of the highest peak the wind was so strong he found he could lie into it without falling. It took his breath away, which mattered little as the vistas now spread out on all sides before his delighted gaze would have done the same job had there not been the slightest whisper of a breeze.

Far below him to the west he had his first view of the little village of Kilmacanogue and as he watched several cars moved up and down through it on the Wicklow road.

To the east was Bray Head, and a ship at sea beyond it created the surreal illusion of sailing along the top of the mountain towards the cross. The golden-thatched roofs and whitewashed walls of the little cottages at the head of Windgates shone in the sunlight and further south the waters of the harbour at Greystones glinted as if spread with floating diamonds.

It was all so beautiful, so wonderfully awe-inspiring that it seemed impossible such things as rows and ructions existed in the same world. How could people be angry or unhappy when there were places like this?

He played with the wind and felt so good.

Janey Mac, what must Holy God feel like looking down on the whole world?

CHAPTER SEVENTEEN

'Sure what could be lovelier than working for God in the church, up there with the priest on the altar? It's something any boy should be proud to do. Don't be mindin' what the trash on the lane say. I'll bring yiz down to see Tommy Kinsella on Monday night.'

The lads felt that the role of altar boy might be considered that of a softie by their cronies and were none too eager to join up, but as usual when Ma decided to go down a particular road there was no turning back, and they duly ended up taking Latin lessons from Tommy Kinsella in the sacristy of the Church of the Most Holy Redeemer every Monday night.

When they had mastered the Latin, or rather memorized it - they hadn't the remotest notion of what any of it meant - they were fitted with the altar boys' rig-out of black soutane that came to the ankles, over which was worn a white lace-trimmed surplice. Dark socks and black canvas runners completed the ensemble. For weddings and on certain holy days a red soutane was worn, so Ma had to fork out for this as soon as she had finished paying for the standard outfit.

The sacristan was a likeable old character called Jemmy Reilly who shuffled about with his elbows sticking out, enquiring of an erring boy if he would 'like a bang on the conk', while raising an arm as if to clout him but never doing so. He kept a small newsagents shop near the church. Whenever he was absent from the sacristy his ghost kept watch over things in the shape of his soutane hanging on the wall, elbows bent as if Jemmy himself were hanging there.

His assistant, John Daly, was a senior altar boy who could step in at any time to serve Mass if someone failed to show up. John would one day inherit Jemmy's job.

Altar boys, the brothers soon learned, were not necessarily angels. They squabbled over who would serve weddings or visiting priests as there was often a few bob of a tip going on such occasions, and there were the wags who would change the opening line of Latin in the Mass from 'Ad deum qui laetificat' to' Ad deum qui le pussycat' just to see the reaction of a visiting cleric.

Being thurifer at benediction was Ray's favourite chore. Benno was nice and short and you just had to stand there in a cloud of sweet-smelling incense swinging the thurible back and forth and, as with the milk-can, resisting the temptation to swing it up and over. A few feet in front of him gleamed the golden tabernacle door which, Dad had informed him, contained grandmother Cranley's wedding ring, donated in response to an appeal many years ago for objects of gold to be melted down for the making of the door.

When they had served their first Mass Ma suggested that the occasion should be marked and preserved by the taking of photographs, and so the cringing pair were instructed to don their altar garb and stand out on the front lawn where any dog or divil might see them, while Dad donned his photographer's hat.

Ma took it all very seriously, making sure Dad wasn't holding the camera baw-ways and warning the lads to stop tittering and 'remember yiz're altar boys, not shaggin' corner boys.'

It has always been a fact of life that if you ask somebody to refrain from giggling you will open his tittering valve to the full and all threats of the consequences will only fuel the frolics, and Ma was not in the least amused when the developed prints revealed a couple of sniggering divils instead of the pious-looking angels she had hoped to capture for posterity.

A monthly duty roster was pinned up in the sacristy and each new notice was earnestly scanned by the altar boys, impatient to know what sort of month lay ahead of them. Some emitted whoops and others moans as their fates were revealed.

A full week of eight o'clock Masses in the depths of winter was no joke. Up at six thirty to walk to Bray in the dark, then straight on to school afterwards. Somehow the early morning darkness wasn't as scary as walking home on a Monday night having served benno at the Miraculous Medal devotions. Ma seldom missed any church function and usually accompanied them home, but one night for some reason she couldn't go. Ray was on duty that night and assured her he would be grand and not to worry, sure didn't he know the road like the back of his hand.

He regretted his bravado as he passed the last of the streetlights that only extended a little way out of the town. He should have asked Dad to come and meet him. By the time he reached the junction where the Soldiers' Road and Killarney Lane intersected he was almost paralysed with fear. Beyond lay Fairy Hill, the loneliest stretch of the road, and now all those ghost stories he had laughed at with the other kids on the way home from school didn't seem funny at all. All manner of horrors stalked his imagination as he stared into the dreadful blackness ahead of him.

At the top of the hill there was an old briar-entangled iron gate that obviously hadn't been opened for donkey's years, and inside that gate was a mysterious, haunted place, overgrown and thorny. Some of the bars of the gate were bent apart just enough to allow a small person access, and now and then just for the thrill of it some intrepid young daredevils would squeeze through and beat their way with stick machetes through the brambles until they came to a strange standing stone with a rough cross hewn on it.

The stone was the last neglected vestige of the ancient Kilsaran church, of which they knew absolutely nothing. It had become to them a curious half-frightening, half-exciting object. What sort of a dicky dido, they asked themselves, would go to the bother of lugging a lump of stone like that to the top of Fairy Hill and planting it there in the middle of a jungle of briars where nobody could see it.

While debating this mystery one day somebody suggested that it might be the work of fairies or the Banshee, and after all, the place was hardly called Fairy Hill for nothing.

This suggestion had an interesting effect on all present. They looked at one another, dropped their sticks and ran scrambling like mad things for the gate, calling for their mammies as they fought to be first out of there.

He stood trembling under the solitary light at the corner of Killarney Lane, and decided to stay where he was until a car came along. Nearby was the small group of new council cottages called Avondale Park. Several of his classmates lived there. Maurice Greene, Freddie Crabbe, Harry Toole. He envied them greatly at this moment. It was past nine o' clock and there was very little traffic on the road.

A good ten minutes had passed and he was shivering with cold as well as fear before he heard a car going down into the hollow at Patchwork and up what they called the New Road, a short concrete-surfaced stretch that had recently bypassed a dangerous bend.

As soon as he caught the first glimpse of the headlamps, he darted off up the hill. He reckoned he could get halfway up before the car caught up with him, and near enough to the top running after it while it lit the road ahead for him.

Oh God! Oh shite!

Suddenly he was left in total darkness.

He stopped dead and looked back to see the red tail lights of the car vanishing into the Soldiers' Road.

The divil skewer yeh anyway, whoever yeh are.

'Oh God, I'm sorry. I'll never do it again.' he whispered.

Just what he would never do again he had no idea, but figured his plight had to be punishment from above for some sin he had forgotten about.

A second car appeared and this time came on up the hill, getting him as far as the side gate of Fairy Hill House before the world returned to blackness. The next stretch would be the worst, along the top of the hill and past the dreaded iron gate. He waited, willing another car to come along, and when none obliged after the longest fifteen minutes imaginable he knew he would somehow have to go on without light.

He got out into the middle of the road and tiptoed along as noiselessly as possible, the little suitcase containing his altar things held at the ready to swing at any would-be assailant.

Coming up to the old gate a sudden rustling in its vicinity sent him whimpering piteously back along the road to the door of Rahan Cottage on the opposite side. There was no footpath and the door opened straight onto the roadside. He was about to ring the bell but stopped himself. How could he let anybody see he was such a cowardy-custard. He would just stand at the door, ready to hammer on it if anything happened, and wait until either a car appeared or somebody from home came looking to see what was keeping him.

Faint sounds came from inside the house. Music. Mr. Woods was listening to his wireless. A kindly old man, Mr. Woods.

With his back to the door and his eyes darting in all directions trying to penetrate the darkness, Ray recalled how a few months back he and Cecil Messitt had pressed the old man's doorbell for divilment on their way home from school. They had run tripping over themselves with laughter down the hill, not stopping to look back until they were near the bottom, and then only to see Mr. Woods calling after them and beckoning them to return to the scene of the crime, which of course they obediently did, despite being sure he wouldn't recognise them at that distance had they continued their chortling flight.

Adults were to be obeyed.

He had taken their names and addresses and a few days later letters arrived at both homes informing the parents of the delinquent behaviour of their offspring.

A Ma like Ma should never be the recipient of such an epistle, and when Ray got in from school she had waved it in his face, holding it in one hand while slapping it with the other as if she were trying to burst a paper bag.

'What's this, eh? What in the name of the sweet Blessed Virgin is the meaning of this?'

There being no answer to that one, he just hung his head and bit his lip.

'The shame of it, letters comin' under the door about a child of mine. Are yeh losin' the bit yeh have or what, to do the like a' that? Frightenin' the life out of a poor old gentleman. It'll be the guards next, as true as Christ it will.'

And she marched him back up Fairy Hill to shamefacedly apologize to Mr. Woods.

Was God now getting his own back?

Car lights flickered on the green wooden fencing back at Fairy Hill House and he pushed himself away from the door, streaking past the iron gate like a cat with a mad dog at its tail. On by the entrance to a big house called Schomberg and then down between the hedgerows and trees of the other side of the hill.

By the time the chugging Hillman Minx sputtered past him he was barrelling along by Boghall corner and the bottom light was in sight.

The highlight of the altar boys' year was a day excursion to Butlin's Holiday Camp at Mosney, for most of them the only journey away from home they were likely to have from one year's end to the other. They travelled, Tommy Kinsella in charge, in a cream-coloured excursion bus hired from Scraggs's Garage. Multi-coloured streamers were purchased in Jemmy Reilly's shop and trailed from the windows of the bus while folk along the way were startled by the noisy yells of the excited trippers as they passed.

A weary and much subdued gang would roll homeward across the flat green meadowlands of Meath, stopping at Balbriggan for the rare treat of a vinegar-drenched bag of chips, in the Cranley boys' case their introduction to this gastronomic delight, chips not making their appearance on Ma's menu until years later.

As a Christmas treat the altar boys were taken to the matinee at the Royal and afterwards to the Kinvara Hotel on the seafront for a meal followed by party games like O'Grady Says and Musical Chairs all presided over by the genial Tommy Kinsella.

Agreeable as these treats were they took second place to the fact that at last they seemed to be doing something that made Ma proud of them.

Ma had not always been a Catholic.

'Bastards!' she whispered hoarsely to Dad late one night, unaware of Ray's cocked ear in his bedroom.

'What?'

'Bastards! Every one of us.'

'What d'yeh mean? Who?'

'Me, Kitty, Noel...the whole shaggin' six of us.'

160

'Begod, yiz're a peculiar clan all right, no doubt about that, but I wouldn't go as far as...'

'Shut up, fool, an' listen. I found somethin' in the trunk, hidden down behind the lining.'

Ray remembered now; earlier in the day Ma had taken the hatchet to the old trunk they had brought from Windgates, the industrious woodworm having rendered it useless for anything other than a good blaze. He had seen the piece of paper flutter out as she had ripped the faded silk lining from the inside, and the look of horror that came over her face as she read it. She had become very quiet for the rest of the day, going about in a world of her own and shaking her head in the manner that mourners at a funeral might be seen to shake their heads in disbelief at the passing of a loved one.

He had asked her what the piece of paper was and she replied that it was nothing as she hastily scrunched it up into a ball, opened the range and flung it in as though it were contaminated with some hideous disease.

A fleeting leap of flame and it was gone.

'Well, what was it then?' Dad asked.

'Mother's marriage certificate,' she answered gravely.

'An' what's wrong with that?'

'Everything's wrong with it. Jesus, Jimmy, they were married in a registry office! I mean, we all knew she had married outside the faith, but good God almighty, a registry office. Sure that's not married at all. It means that none of us came into the world...you know... properly like. All bastards an' Mother never mentioned it. What in the name a' God are we goin' to do now? We'll probably never see heaven.'

161

'Sure yiz can't blame yourselves for the like a' that. Yiz knew nothin' about it an' had nothin' to do with it.'

'Bastards never do,' she replied dejectedly.

Ray was becoming more and more confused. Ma was referring to herself and Kitty as bastards! How the flippin' hell could that be? Surely bastards were boys who had been very bold, in the same way that bitches were naughty girls. He was fecked if he could figure it out. And what was a registry office anyway?

Grandmother had been ecumenically far ahead of her time, and as a teenager had left Greystones to work in Dublin where she met and married Thomas James, a Protestant. They lived in the North Circular gate lodge of the Phoenix Park where he was a park ranger and was in charge of opening and closing the gates. Unfortunately he was also fond of opening the bottle and could be cruelly violent when in drink.

When grandmother went into labour with Ma, her fourth child, she boarded a tram outside the park gates to take her to the hospital, but should have caught an earlier one, and so it transpired that Ma was born on the footplate of an old Dublin tram outside the Rotunda Hospital in the midsummer of 1910.

She often told the kids' of her terror at the thundering roar of the machine gun that was mounted on the roof of the lodge during the 1916 Rising, and how its bullets had hopped on the road about her mother's feet one day as she tried to get to O'Connor's shop outside the gates for a candle. An officer had come on the scene and ordered them to cease fire immediately and had escorted grandmother safely to the shop and back, apologizing and promising that the trigger-happy boyos on the roof would be severely disciplined.

All of this, coupled with the fear of a drunken father, didn't make Ma's childhood sound like an enviable one, and yet she could speak with fondness of her years in the Park, playing among the flower-beds of the People's Gardens or running up and down the steps of the Wellington Monument and quenching her thirst at the fountains.

Then when she was seven years old her father had died, leaving grandmother with six young children and no home. The lodge had to be vacated to make way for grandfather's successor. They managed to rent a couple of dingy rooms in a tenement at 5 Montpelier Hill nearby, thanks to the generosity of Mrs. Lonergan who had recently taken over O'Connor's shop, The Old Toll House.

They lived for sixteen years in those rooms in the poorest of circumstances. Grandmother got a job at the munitions factory in Parkgate Street but the few shillings it paid barely allowed them to exist, and soon their bits and pieces began to vanish into the pawnshop, often never to be redeemed.

During most of those years there were empty rooms in the cottage at Windgates, its only occupants being grandmother's sister Lizzie and their father, Tom 'The Horn' Byrne. Lizzie, feeling disinclined to forgive and forget her sister's earlier waywardness, was reluctant to invite her back into the fold and decided to let her stew in her own juice. She did, however, take some of the children during their school holidays, and in 1926 when old Tom died aged 93, she decided to keep Kitty with her for company, an act for which Kitty never forgave her.

Kitty loved Dublin and was still attending school at sixteen years of age which was unusual in times when most young people found themselves of necessity pushed into any kind of work they could find at thirteen or fourteen. More than half a century after Lizzie's death in 1933, Kitty was still vilifying her to anyone who would listen.

Only when Lizzie was dying did Grandmother and the rest of the family escape from the misery of the tenements to the fields and farmlands of Windgates where they could at least be poor in the comfort of their own home, and where a restless night could be soothed by a glance out the back window, down over the dark rolling fields to where the sea was transformed by the rising moon to a sheet of exquisite silver.

Grandmother had all of her children converted to the Catholic faith some years after their father died, and Ma grew up to be living proof that none can surpass the convert for zeal.

CHAPTER EIGHTEEN

Something very peculiar was going on. The older kids were all worked up about some new musical phenomenon. Girls gathered in groups on the Lane and chattered excitedly about the latest breed of heartthrob that was capturing their hearts and imaginations.

'What's all the commotion about?' he had enquired of Bridgie Hughes one day up the buildings.

Bridgie was about fourteen. She stared at him in disbelief and replied in an accent usually only heard at the pictures:

'You tellin' me you ain't never heard of Bill Haley? Crazy, man, crazy!'

She wiggled off snapping her fingers.

'See ya later, alligator!'

Ah, for feck sake! What's got into them all? They're even talkin' like the cowboys.

There had been many heartthrobs before, of course; Ma said Bing Crosby was a heartthrob. But this was different. This time it wasn't just the singers; it was the new wild music that all these characters with strange-sounding names were playing.

Rock 'n' Roll they called it.

It thumped and roared from the wireless in glorious abandon, bringing with it its own language which the teenagers latched onto much to the horror of their parents, who were informed in no uncertain terms that they were square, unhip and just plain not with it.

Not with what? They wondered.

The very fact that older folk didn't like Rock 'n' Roll was enough to make the kids realize they had something of their own; something no other generation of teenagers had experienced.

Their very own music.

Something they could discuss among themselves and overhearing parents wouldn't understand anyway.

'It's what yeh call scat singin',' Dad informed them.

'Deed an' it's not singin' at all!' Ma snorted. 'Eejits shoutin' an' roarin' their bloody guts out.'

She would yell at them to 'turn that infernal racket down before I put the shaggin' brush through it' whenever it blared forth from the daring little wireless.

Whatever it was, Ray wanted to be part of all the excitement, but being only twelve and Rock 'n' Roll being the domain of teenagers, he could only live on the fringe and lap up the overflow for now. When he turned thirteen he would shout it from the top of Sugarloaf.

Sitting against a haycock he watched the big girls jiving in Butler's field to a portable gramophone while they sang along with their idols. As they whirled, their wide flared skirts spun up and out around them like the rings of Saturn, exposing white thighs, pink suspenders and the occasional glimpse of variously hued knickers.

'Don't be cruel,' they pleaded, and 'Don't step on my blue suede shoes.'

When they sang about bald-headed Sally's boyfriend, the deceiving Uncle John, ducking back in the alley, they leaned so far back they were almost horizontal, only to be jerked upright again by their partners just when serious injury appeared inevitable.

He listened as they drooled over photographs in a magazine of a sulky looking Rock 'n' Roller who went by the curious name of Elvis Presley. They said the quarest things about him!

He was 'real cool', 'real gone', 'the most' and 'the livin' end'.

One girl remarked: 'Ooh, Jaysus will yeh look at them come-to-bed eyes! Wouldn't yeh just love to...yeh know.'

What in the name a' God were they pratin' about? Love to what?

There was obviously some secret, delicious and mysterious, about being a teenager, and he wanted to grow up as soon as possible, God, if you please.

The girls stopped dancing as a horse pulling a hay bogey came rattling and jingling into the field from the old track beside the orchard. They ran with the lads to jump on the low flat bogey, the back of which almost touched the ground, for a bumpy ride across the field, then watched the man throw a heavy rope around a haycock and commence winching it aboard. The big ratchet sounded like a giant corncrake as he pulled the long wooden lever back and forth.

The haycock began to inch forward. Sweat gleamed on the sunburned arms of the man as he worked. The kids observed in sunny silence a musty-smelling circle of dead grass being slowly revealed as the cock moved eclipse-like across its resting place and onto the sloping boards of the bogey.

When it was secured and moving away as many youngsters as could fit clambered on board and leaned against the warm hay, heedless of the shouts of the driver to 'get off to hell outa that before yiz's all kilt', while the unlucky ones ran alongside still hoping for a place.

'Move over there, Noel, an' let's up.'

'I can't, there's no room.'

'Ah, 'mup outa me way for feck sake, there's loadsa room. Here Con, give us a hoosh up.'

'Go 'way! I wanta get up there meself.'

'Feck yeh for a louser, then.'

'I'm tellin' yer mammy yer cursin',' someone threatened.

'Go on an' tell her then, yeh mouth yeh, I don't give a shite.'

A chorus of singsong name-calling broke out.

'Cranley the banley the ricksticks manley.'

'Carrby the barrby the ricksticks marrby.'

'Healy the bealy the ricksticks mealy.'

The noisy crew rode as far as the farm gateway to Darby's Lane before jumping off and straggling back to the field to await the bogey's return. Several of the haycocks were almost levelled, resisting the sheer delight of frolicking on them being too much for any normal kid.

'I'm the king idda castle, Get down yeh dirty rascal!'

Whoever was on top defended his or her lofty throne against all comers until he or she was dislodged and sent head over heels to the stubbly ground. When the cock was demolished, its ropes and stones lying among the scattered remains, the young wreckers raced one another to be first on top of the next undisturbed cock.

Cousin Marie and her younger sister Mona too were bitten by the Rock 'n' Roll bug, and on frequent visits to Redford with Val - frequent probably because Aunt Molly always gave them the price of the pictures at the Ormonde in Greystones - Ray got to know the names and sounds of people like Fats Domino, whose voice sounded as fat as his name as he sang about Blueberry Hill or how good life would be when his Dreamboat came home; Bill Haley who rocked around the clock and invited everybody to Razzle Dazzle, and the Platters with their crystal-toned renderings of The Great Pretender and Only You. Elvis Presley was seldom far from the turntable, informing his adoring fans that they were nothin' but hound dogs.

Already the first Rock 'n' Roll film was doing the rounds. It was built around the Bill Haley hit Rock around the Clock and teenagers were coming home from the cinema breathlessly telling of ushers unable to control the audience or prevent them from leaving their seats and dancing in the aisles.

No particular singer at this time had made any great impression on Ray but it was impossible not to be caught up in all the hurly-burly and the air of expectancy that prevailed; an eager anticipation of what might come next, and a feeling that this was just the beginning of something really extraordinary.

The radio programmes were still dominated by what were considered by fans of the new music to be boring old crooners and dance bands, but their days were numbered. Although there were as yet relatively few Rock 'n' Roll stars it was inevitable, given the unprecedented success and excitement surrounding these pioneers, that they would be followed by a host of other young rockers who would rapidly take over the airwaves with devastating consequences for the tired old idols of their parents.

One or two of the not-so-ancient ones made some embarrassing attempts at crossing over to Rock 'n' Roll and in some cases even had hits in the new idiom, but for them it was a last gasp before being overwhelmed. Even Bill Haley, the man credited with starting it all, was found wanting in wildness and exposed as 'one of them pretending to be one of us'. His watered-down versions of numbers like 'Shake, Rattle and Roll' were shown up by Presley's use of the original and, for the time, daring lyrics.

Rock 'n' Roll was not going to be insipid.

Rock 'n' Roll was going to musically thump the ears of the western world, sending the 1950s reeling and rocking into history as the decade that heralded the dawn of a new era of music that pulsed with the beat of life itself, giving the young a voice of their own for the first time. Its repercussions would be felt around the globe, and in Ballywaltrim its early stirrings were felt and welcomed among the haycocks in Butler's field.

There was a new baby at number fifteen. Ma, at forty-six years of age, had given birth to her sixth child, a boy called Gabriel who did his best to outroar Rock 'n' Roll.

Neighbours said wasn't she a great woman.

It was a time of crazes, all of which, with the exception of Rock 'n' Roll, would come and go in a matter of months. Every youngster had to have a Davy Crockett coonskin cap, and mothers were badgered into making them up from old fur coats and hats. It was considered advisable at the height of this particular craze to keep a watchful eye on the family cat.

Hundreds of enthusiasts flocked to the Royal cinema when a chap called Billy Panama appeared on stage there. He was the world champion yo-yo player and gave a live demonstration during a craze for the humble yo-yo.

Ronnie Delaney won a gold medal for Ireland at the Olympics and people said wasn't it great the way he went down on his knees and thanked God in front of the whole pagan world.

Refugees arrived in Bray from the Hungarian Uprising, and one of them, a chap called Fuchs, was made a bit of a celebrity when he joined the pupils at St. Cronan's.

Boys sat on top of Hodson's wall sucking ice lollies from Andy's while they watched a building under construction at the lonely fork in the road at Hollybrook.

'It's goin' to be a garage, me daddy says.'

'Nah! Who'd build a feckin' garage way out here?'

Becoming bored, they dropped the wall, hanging on by their fingertips before letting go, landing nimbly on the roadside and straggling homewards in the heat.

And there was talk of girls. None of the lads knew what, but there was something about girls; something that gave them strange thrills as they sat in the field debating various things they had heard, things they thought they knew, about girls. They guessed wildly at the nature of the female function in life and were surprised at how merely talking about it had the same effect on the whole gang.

'Dirty' was the word they used for it because they knew of no other. What they did know, through priest and parents, was that anything to do with the human body between the navel and the knee was dirty, and the mickey being bang in the middle of this zone it stood to reason that the thoughts that affected it so acutely and the sensations those thoughts produced were dirty.

Hidden by the long grass in the pond field, they were in the middle of a particularly juicy discussion when one of the gang announced:

'My mickey's up!'

'So's Mine!'

'Let's see.'

'I will an' me shite.'

'Ah, go on, giz a geck outa that, yeh louser of a fraidycat.'

'You first, then, seein' as yer so smart.'

'Right, I will. There y'are, see?'

Soon half a dozen pairs of trousers lay discarded in the grass and half a dozen mickies stared at the sunny sky while they were compared and admired. Someone said it was a mortal sin, but nobody made a move to cover up.

'I wonder do young-ones do this.'

'How could they, yeh dopey eejit? Girls don't have mickies. Why do yeh think they're called empty-forks?'

'Ah, you me granny. I didn't mean that. I meant do young-ones take their knickers off when they're out together like us?'

'Ooh, stop, will yeh. Hey! Who's on for a run around the field in our skins?'

Six Sloppy Joes joined the bundle of trousers.

'Have a decko before we stand up. Yeh never know what oul' tickle-the-bricks might be hangin' around.'

Heads appeared above the grass like swivelling periscopes.

'Not a sinner. Let's go. We'll run as far as the ditch an' back.'

They leapt up and charged across the field, giggling and whooping as dog daisies and tall grasses tickled parts unaccustomed to being tickled by grass or anything else.

When they had dressed again and the little gang started back up the fields towards the cottages, Ray headed off in the opposite direction saying he had tuppence and was going to spend it in Harris's shop at Kilcroney. In fact he hadn't a copper to his name.

He climbed through the gap near the pond onto the tree-shaded back road and at the hairpin bend climbed into Pembroke Wood. Following one of the many paths he went deep into the wood, passing the stout hanging vines and broken vegetation that marked the spot where they sometimes played Tarzan. Swinging up among the high boughs on those vines was the biggest thrill imaginable.

Up until now.

He stood in a little clearing that allowed the sunshine to beam in. His heart thumped and his whole body shook, and he realized, he was committing the biggest, mortalest sin ever as unbelievable sensations exploded inside him and then receded leaving a vast emptiness into which poured fearsome black floods of guilt.

He was sobbing as he fixed his clothes, telling God he was sorry and promising from the bottom of his heart never to do the like of that again. He prayed for forgiveness all the way home, only breaking the string of Hail Marys to quench his thirst at the fountain near the hairpin bend.

All his fervent pledges were, alas, feathers in a tempest when confronted with the urgency of life itself, and time and time again they were renewed only to be blown uselessly aside by the next overwhelming onslaught.

Streaking sessions with the boys became regular events until one day somebody spotted them and dutifully informed the parents. The two lads escaped the full rigour of Ma's temper due to the lucky fact that Jack and Chris were due home on holiday that very day. The sheer wickedness of the story she had been told left Ma speechless with disbelief, and before she found her voice the visitors were at the gate, so she made do with mortifying the pair of 'divils unhung' in front of them, asking their opinion of boys who would take their trousers off and go tearing around the fields, daring Holy God to strike them dead on the spot.

'What, I ask yiz, in the name of the Blessed Virgin Mary could have possessed them to get up to such evil carry-on?

The visitors looked bemused. Jack muttered something about boys being boys and she retorted that it was nothing less than sheer filth, that they were divils of the deepest dye, and would have to confess their disgusting sin against purity to a priest as quick as ever they could in order to cleanse their blackened souls and get back into the state of grace. And to think that the same little gets do be up there on the altar with the holy priests!

Streaking now being too risky the curious young-lads turned their unholy attention to the seeking out of 'lies'. Lies consisted of flattened areas of grass in long meadows, behind ditches, in the woods and bushes; anywhere courting couples mistakenly believed themselves hidden from prying eyes. They were usually searched for on Mondays and stealthily revisited at the weekend.

A much-favoured spot by young lovers was the Dargle Glen, a beautiful oak-wooded ravine about a mile from Ballywaltrim as the crow flies or boys travel. The Bray River tumbled through the glen casting countless diamonds into the sunlight as it thundered over great boulders on its way to the sea at Bray. The place had been a major tourist attraction in Georgian and Victorian times, but had declined in popularity with the advent of the motorcar, which allowed trippers to travel much farther afield from their holiday base at the seaside town.

It was now largely only visited by locals and courting couples, some of whom came out on the bus from Dublin to Enniskerry and walked down Lover's Leap Lane into the Glen. For the young cowboys and Indians of Ballywaltrim it was a rugged canyon straight out of the Wild West.

The kids soon got to know which couples 'did it', and the ones who didn't were deemed hopeless and left alone. A good lie could provide entertainment all through the summer months, or until one of the peeping Toms thought it a clever idea to let a Tarzan-like yell out of him at the crucial moment, causing a mad scramble for clothes and much cursing on the part of the unfortunate victims. The culprits knew they were safe, a man with his trousers round his ankles being in no state to give chase, and even if he did, sure didn't they know the whole glen like their own back gardens and would lose the dirty brute no bother.

An afternoon spent watching a lie was far more interesting than going to the pictures where the Chap never got any further than kissin' his mot before the feckin' picture faded out.

CHAPTER NINETEEN

As he and Cecil Messitt stuffed golden rustling heaps of dry November leaves into sacks on the back road, Ray for the first time in his short life felt a twinge of nostalgic sadness at the passing of time. They had been playing at burying each other under huge piles of leaves to see who could stay under longest. Even on the coldest day, a few minutes in the leafy tomb and you were sweatin' buckets, just like being buried in the hay in Darley's barn.

The crisp late-autumn sunlight filtered down through the near-naked branches of the trees as they mingled to form an arboreous tunnel above the road, and the sweet smell of wood-smoke drifted across from the chimney of Paddy Woodcock's little gate lodge at Violet Hill.

1957 was on the way out.

He felt it had been a good year; a warm, friendly year, and he had an uneasy feeling about leaving it. Even the number fifty-seven had a homely warmth to it.

There had been many endings and beginnings, many changes.

Not that everything had been rosy at home, in fact financially it had been one of the worst years the family had ever endured. Dad had lost his job at the convent, word being sent to the house one day as he lay in bed with the 'flu that he needn't bother going back to work anymore.

It was a devastating blow. He had never been out of work before, and even the thought of applying for the dole, being handed forms he couldn't fill in, must have been a daunting prospect.

It was heartbreaking to see him sit with pen and paper to practice writing his name. He was so clever about so many things, possessing a quiet sort of wisdom of his own, that Ray was sure he could easily learn to read if he put his mind to it.

After some months during which the family would have gone hungry but for the kindness of O'Regan's in allowing Ma to run up a huge bill at the small grocery shop near the Town Hall, Dad was delighted when Father Breen offered him some work at the graveyard.

'Thanks be to the Sacred Heart an' his Blessed Mother!' Ma said on hearing the good news. 'Didn't I tell yiz God is good.'

It was as happy a week as they had had for many a long month and when Friday finally arrived Dad called at the presbytery and told Father Breen he was there to collect his 'few bob'.

The reverend gentleman looked at him in astonishment.

'Good God, Jimmy, I couldn't pay you money while you are drawing the dole! I just thought you'd be glad of something to occupy your time while you are idle.'

Ma was livid.

'What the hell d'yeh mean, he won't give yeh anything? Go back down there an' get yer wages that you've worked all week for.'

Ma, of course, had the money already spent, or rather allocated to division among the most urgent of the bills. When it finally sank in that there was no hope, that you

178

couldn't very well argue with a priest, she sat down and cried bitterly.

'What's this rotten world comin' to in the name a' God, when a priest can do the like a' that on poor people an' we without bit, bite or sup in the house?'

It was one of the very few occasions on which she looked and sounded beaten.

On the eighteenth of February Ray had at last entered the long anticipated world of the teenager, and during the lazy summer months had often walked Gina Turner up the road to Andy's. They had both just finished primary school, and as if to establish beyond all doubt that the pair of them were a perfect match, both had come second in their respective Primary Cert. exams.

Then one day the world showed its true colours when some kids on the Lane gleefully informed him that they had seen Gina going up to Andy's with Noel Healy.

Feck that for a game of cowboys.

In his misery he bombarded Heaven with requests for help, and not for the first time God, Saint Anthony and the whole gang of them sitting cushy up there let him down.

He had received the incredible sum of twelve shillings as a prize for his success in the Primary. Ma added something to it, God knows how, and bought him an accordion, an instrument in which he had as much interest as a chicken has in Tuesday, but out of which Dad could knock quite a few tunes.

He had hinted timorously that a guitar might be more acceptable, but the idea was so outlandish to Ma that he might as well have asked for Nelson's Pillar.

With Dad out of work the squeezebox soon found its way into O'Carroll's pawnshop. It reappeared twice but like the drowning man failed to resurface the third time and was never squeezed again in Ballywaltrim.

From the crowded footbridge near the railway station he had watched the last steam train chuff out of Bray. No tears would be shed by the oul' ones whose kids dared one another to stand directly over the funnels of engines passing underneath, resulting in gangs of little Al Jolsons going home to Mammies who could be forgiven for thinking that the black babies they had 'bought' had arrived to claim their places in the family.

Bray, as it did every summer, overflowed with visitors. The trains disgorged them in droves to hustle and bustle their way along the narrow, teeming Albert Walk, chock-a-block with little souvenir shops, pongo halls and amusement arcades with juke boxes blaring out the latest hits. There were as many accents in the air as there were colours in the hundreds of plastic windmills and beach balls that hung above the heads of the milling holidaymakers.

He spent a lot of time around the seafront that summer, and in a small arcade called The Manhattan he finally lost his heart - and a fair bit of his soul - to Rock 'n' Roll. The jukebox stood at the far end of the arcade, a multicoloured monarch lording it over the two rows of one-armed bandits and pinball machines, and the kids in Ray's age group hung around while the visitors and older teenagers pumped their tanners and shillings into the slot.

One particular disc stood out in the neat black rows of 78s by reason of the fact that it was white. It was white not because of some deviation from the norm in the manufacturing process, but as a result of being played countless times more than any other record in the machine, sometimes being selected half a dozen consecutive times before another song got a look in.

And he knew why.

From the top of his head to the tips of his tingling toes he knew why, but could never have explained it. He didn't even know which instruments were being played in that rolling intro, nor did he care. All he knew was that he felt it in every nerve in his body.

And then the voice came in; a voice that so naturally matched and blended with the sound it was the very essence of the newborn music:

'A-well-a bless my soul, what's wrong with me...'

So this is what they've all been raving about! Holy feck!

Looking around the arcade he saw young bodies bopping as they played the slots and pinball machines, and others outside the doors breaking into short bursts of dance as they passed up and down Albert Walk. He wanted to join in but was too shy.

The same record was played white in the big arcades on the seafront, The Fun Palace at the southern end and Dawson's at the foot of Bray Head, and sometimes he would run the length of the prom, a mile of blue railing on the seaward side and a mile of blue seating hidden under a mile of visiting bottoms on the other, just to hear the song from as many jukeboxes as possible on the same day.

He had to have that record.

At home where he could play it for himself. To actually own and control that magic sound.

He had heard Elvis Presley before, of course, singing things like 'Don't be Cruel' and 'Blue Suede Shoes', but these just hadn't registered in the way that the latest one, 'All Shook Up', had. The only explanation he could come up with as to why this had been the case was that he had simply been too young.

Jakers, he was glad he was thirteen!

He would save every ha'penny until he could afford the record. He did the weekly shopping for Ma on Saturday mornings and she gave him a tanner for that, although it was hard earned lugging the heavy message bags home from Bray. Dinny Byrne and his horse had retired from Caulfield's and Ma now did most of her shopping at O'Regan's.

Often, as he trudged homewards laden down with groceries, he wondered why the hell God had to go and plonk Fairy Hill between Ballywaltrim and Bray.

Slowly, painfully slowly, the little pile of coins on the bedroom mantelpiece - tanners, thrupenny bits, coppers and even a shilling - grew until they added up to the magic sum of five and ninepence, the amount required for the purchase of the much-desired piece of wax.

Heavy of pocket and light of heart, he entered Murdoch's shop on Main Street where the assistant slipped the record out of its cover for inspection. The grooves gleamed in shiny black perfection as he expertly twirled it around on his thumb and forefinger before wrapping it between two sheets of corrugated cardboard, and Ray happily anticipated the thousands of times he would play it before it turned white. The dog listening at the horn of an old gramophone on the HMV label he was familiar with from some of Dad's old records, but they were generally drab grey-black creations whereas this new record sported a label of bold rebellious red. He handed over his heap of small change. The man counted it and gave him ninepence back.

'Five bob'll do the job,' he said.

'Yeah? Oh, thanks! Thanks very much!'

It was his day all right. Janey, he could have had it a week ago if he had known he was going to get it at that price. Very nice of that fella.

He was hurrying back up the street with his treasure under his oxter when he remembered he hadn't bought the box of gramophone needles Dad had given him a shilling for. He crossed over to Nolan's electrical shop and waited impatiently while some customers ahead of him were served.

Come on, come on!

He willed Mr. Nolan to get a move on. He couldn't wait to lay that precious disc on the soft brown felt of the turntable. A thrill rolled over him as he contemplated his ownership of 'All Shook Up' and he chuckled to himself, giving the record a squeeze.

There was a dull snapping sound and he choked on his chuckle, the thrill turning to one of horror.

He had broken enough of Dads records years ago to know that his prized Presley disc had snapped across like a big biscuit. He stumbled out of the shop close to tears and started for home in a state of shock, oblivious to everyone and everything except the awful calamity that had befallen him.

183

What would he say?

What in the name of all the divils in hell was he going to tell them all? He had been boasting about getting it for days, and now people were bound to want to come in and hear it on the gramophone, and here it was, brand new and banjaxed.

Shite, shite, shite!

It was the most miserable walk home he had ever undertaken.

'D'yeh want a jaunt home, Raymond?'

He jumped. He had been so lost in his mental search for the best course of action that he hadn't noticed Jimmy Jones coming along behind him in the horse and dray he drove for Whites. He crossed the road and pulled himself aboard the dray. Jimmy had been on his rounds collecting slop for the pigs and the sour stink of half-rotten household waste mingled with the smell of the manure that coated the floor and sides. The combined stench was truly awesome.

Jimmy prated away to him as the dray creaked along behind the trotting horse, but he heard nothing of it.

'Have yeh got somethin' stuck in yer guggle or what? I might as well be talkin' to oul' Dolly there, bejaysus!'

Ray forced a grin.

The dray stopped to let him off before it turned into white's drive, and as he made his unhappy way up the Lane he decided he would feign surprise when he opened the bag at home; pretend to be knocked bandy with the shock.

'Well, are yeh happy now?' Ma asked, looking up from blackleading the range as he came in.

'Yeah!' he replied with a delighted smile that cost him dearly.

He opened the bag and drew out a black half moon.

'It's broken!' he cried, not really needing to put much effort into his act.

'It's what?' Ma snapped.

He held up the half moon.

'Did yeh drop the bloody thing on the road or what?'

'No,' he answered truthfully.

'Well, yeh better get back down there an' get it exchanged as quick as yeh can.'

It was an order.

'He gave me ninepence off,' he muttered, not knowing what he hoped to gain by this revelation.

'A-course he did, the cutehawk! Why wouldn't he, an' he goin' to pocket your five shillin's?'

'I don't think they exchange records, there's a notice...'

'Don't talk bosh,' she interrupted. 'They'll have to exchange it, fathead. What the hell good is a broken record, even if there is only a dose of mad screechin' on it?'

He hadn't expected this, but he should have. He should have known Ma would take a sheep's head back to the butcher's if it looked crooked at her.

'Get goin' now, an' don't come back here without either a new record or your money back. I don't know why yeh were such a stumor not to check it before yeh left the shop anyway. I'll never bloody teach yiz.'

She resumed her blackleading.

'Sure they'll be closed now,' he said, thankfully indicating the clock, which obligingly chimed five as he spoke.

'Well, see that yeh do it on Monday then. I'm tellin' yeh, yeh couldn't be up to these people. Robbers and besters everywhere.'

'Yeah, all right. I will.'

Relief. Off the hook for the time being.

Before the weekend was over everyone in the lane knew about his record-breaking misfortune, and even when he went up the road to the shop Mary Murphy asked him about it. Mary's mother had opened a little shop when Andy's closed down for good earlier in the year. Murphy's also closed after a short period leaving Ballywaltrim shopless, and the kids were obliged to take their sweaty pennies down through the fields and woods to Foster's who had taken over Harris's at Kilcroney.

Monday rolled around and he was still without a solution to his problem. He couldn't very well go back to the shop, and if he told Ma the truth she would probably mazzle him. On the other hand if he didn't produce a new record or the money she would probably go for him anyway, or worse still, go down to the shop herself. He winced at the thought.

For more than two hours he sat in the Little Wood near Boghall corner, having said he was on his way to Murdoch's. He spent the time scouring his mind for a way out, and eventually went home and told Ma that the man who sold him the record was on holidays and wouldn't be back for two weeks.

The lie saved his skin, and after a few more fibs and dodges Ma's interest flagged and died. She never did get to know the truth. Meanwhile, the first time he found himself alone in the house, Ma having taken Rita and Val to their Irish dancing class with the others in tow, he took the record out and examined it. The chunk that had broken away had left about half an inch of groove near the centre.

He wound the gramophone and lifted the lid, releasing the pleasant woody smell that reminded him of times past, then placed the disc, or rather what had once been a disc, on the turntable. He inserted a new needle and dropped the used one into the little chrome receptacle set into the wood beside the turntable for that purpose, and carefully lifted the heavy sound box in his right hand while pushing the speed control to seventy eight with his left.

He lowered the needle.

The kitchen was instantly pulsating with the final throbbing chorus of 'All Shook Up'. He jumped and capered around the room, completely possessed by the sound, which in the close confines of the kitchen seemed even louder than the jukeboxes.

Thirty ecstatic seconds it lasted, then sudden silence except for the wavy crackling as the needle went weaving in and out, trapped at the end of the groove. He lifted the sound box and played the half-inch of song again. And a third time.

He ran out the back door and around to the side window to hear it from there, galloped back in and put it on yet again. He pranced around like a loolah until, exhausted and dizzy, he flopped down into the armchair.

Wheee! Rock 'n' Roll was here to stay!

Ma didn't take to Elvis at all; said he looked like a bloody corner-boy with his slicked-back hair. Old Mrs. Ryan called in one day and on seeing a picture of him that Ray had hung on the wall remarked to Ma on his 'lovely come-to-bed eyes'. Ma drew a deep breath and gave a little snort of disgust, but said nothing until the old lady had gone.

'Wouldn't yeh think, now, that an oul' one of her years would have more sense than to be comin' out with the like a' that in front of the children. Anyway,' she turned to Ray, 'I don't know why yeh have that thing stuck up there. D'yeh think Elvis Presley gives a shite about you? If he came up the lane tomorrow he wouldn't look at yeh, an' you, like the poor fool yeh are, flitterin' good money away on his rotten records, makin' him rich. Will yeh for Christ's sake get a bitta sense. An' get that shaggin' hair cut or I'll drag yeh down to Jemmy Doran's by it.'

Like most of the lads in the Lane, he had taken to combing his hair back into a D.A., and to do it properly a fairly long growth was required. Ma liked to see the boys' hair cut 'up to the lumps', which was no use at all when it came to the D.A.

He wondered did she know it stood for duck's arse.

Ma's disapproval of Rock 'n' Roll didn't stop him listening to it, any more than her disapproval of the library had prevented him joining.

The ructions there had been over that!

'Feckin' bookworms were never any use. I know all about it. You're Uncle Tit was a bookworm an' what good was it to him? Goin' around scutterin' about things nobody else in the house could shaggin'-well understand. Yeh'll never get anywhere mopin' around with yer snot stuck in a book, so yeh can get that library business out of yer head. Books are no good to me!'

Uncle Tit was her brother, Tommy, who had been nicknamed Tomtit as a child and unhappily for him the latter bit stuck. He was now a soldier living in County Kildare and usually referred to by Ma as 'the lad on the Curragh'.

Ray loved his visits to the library, searching the shelves for books on space and the nature of the universe, a subject that fascinated him. These were few and far between, but the kindly librarian, Máirín Byrne, who was seldom seen without a warm smile on her face, got to know his preferences and would keep them aside for him whenever they became available.

His enthusiasm for so 'weird' a subject was further fired by the much-publicised arrival of the space age; the Russian Sputnik was up there now whirling around the planet, bleeping away all the arguments of the many who were of the opinion that space was a figment of some mad scribes imagination, a load of makey-uppy moonshine. He had been ridiculed by some of his schoolmates when he tried to convince them that their world really was 'one of them roundy planet yokes'.

'Gerraway, yeh feckin' eejit, sure yeh on'y have to look to see that it's flat exceptin' the mountains!'

Mr. Donegan had wasted his time teaching them about Columbus. It was roundy for school, but not really.

Before leaving St. Cronan's he and three others from his class were picked to represent their school at an inter-schools question time held in the Little Flower Hall, and here his extraterrestrial curiosity paid off by enabling him to answer a fluke question which in turn helped his school beat the Greystones Christian Brothers team. Mr. Donegan beamed and the Brothers scowled; it didn't look good for a CBS to be hammered by a mere lay National School.

'How would you say a tin of food is sealed?' the question master asked.

By lucky coincidence Ray had been reading of how future space travellers would eat their rations from hermetically sealed containers. He was by no means sure this was the answer, but it was worth a try.

'Her-met-ically,' he staggered the word out, and waited for the hall to disintegrate with laughter. To his surprise his reply was greeted with dead silence from the crowd, and only when the man said 'Correct' did they cheer and clap, leaving him with the impression that, like himself, they hadn't the foggiest idea what the word meant.

Each contestant was expected to sing a song and when his turn came he strode over to the mike and launched into a recent number one hit called 'Young Love.' There being no accompaniment, he cheerfully began about two keys too high and his singing debut ended in an undignified squawk when the soaring chorus came around.

He slunk back mortified to his chair and sat with his team-mates, Maurice Greene, Leo Temple and Gerry Sayers who had just delivered a rousing rendition of Johnnie Ray's 'Walkin' in the Rain.'

There was a ripple of sympathetic applause as 'Young Love' died.

Himself and Con Carr washed up and peeled potatoes in Borza's Sunshine Cafe on the seafront towards the end of the summer holidays, and for the first time he had a little pocket money of his own. The pair of them whizzed up and down the hills, Ray on Ma's An Tóstal bike, yelling their favourite songs as they pedalled to work. Ma had gone head, neck and ears in debt again to get the bike on the Kathleen Mavourneen.

In September he began his spell at Bray Technical School, one of only two pupils from his class at St. Cronan's to do so, Cecil Messitt from number eight being the other.

There were girls at the Tech. Some of the girls were still just girls, others were blossoming into lovely young women. Oh, God, they were feckin' gorgeous! But the lovelier they were the more shy and awkward he felt, and he became angry at his inability to hold a simple conversation with any of them without becoming as dumb as a church bell on Good Friday.

And then there was Miss Meagher, the principal's daughter, who was in charge of Physical Training. On Wednesday afternoons she stood on the high stage in the gym dressed entirely in bright green, her shapely legs soaring heavenwards under the shortest skirt he had ever seen.

During one PT session as the boys lined up to do handstands he was paying a little too much attention to Miss Meagher and not enough to lining up. They were down on all fours and when she gave the word dozens of pairs of heels were thrown into the air. Having carelessly placed himself too close to the line of students in front of him, one of the heels, that of one Victor Cantwell, smashed into the bridge of his nose. He was stunned and suddenly there was blood everywhere.

Victor stared in alarm from behind his specs. Then, like an Irish cousin of Nyoka the Jungle Girl, the green goddess leapt from the stage. She told him to hold his head back, put her arm around his shoulder and steered him along the corridor to the toilets where she dabbed his damaged snout with cold water and cleaned him up as best she could.

As the initial shock receded he found himself quite enjoying her soothing attentions. Her flaming hair fell around his face as she closely examined the wound. She smelled nice too, sending his mind back to Nurse Blakely.

The only time he ever mitched from school was the afternoon he and Cecil skipped PT and went to see Elvis Presley in 'Loving You' at the Royal, and judging by the length of the queue and the age group it consisted of it was evident that there was a sizeable upsurge in school absenteeism that day.

It was a strange experience. Girls screamed as soon as Presley appeared on the screen, and screamed again every time he whipped and whirled his legs and hips around in an extraordinary manner as he belted out songs that had liberally sprinkled the charts that year. Heads bobbed up and down in the darkness of the cinema. Some people stood up and clapped along. Others got out into the aisles and began jiving. Eventually the only way to see the screen was by standing up and soon the whole cinema was on its feet.

The usher, Jo-Jo Hamilton, made some vain attempts to restore order, then, as far as his job would allow, he gave up and joined in the fun. For most of those present the film provided their introduction to jeans and denim, tight jeans and a jacket of that material being the attire of the character played by their hero, and it became every young-lad's ambition to own such an outfit. They would have to wait, even those older ones who might be able to afford them, as jeans had not made their appearance in the shops generally yet.

The carnival in the Carlisle Grounds neared the end of its annual visit and as the evenings drew in it was an exciting place to be when all the coloured lights came on and the loudspeakers blared the big hits of the summer into the starry air above the jingle jangle of the of the funfair. In a swing-boat he and Ronnie Turner pulled on the ropes like a couple of demented bell-ringers, each standing up in turn as the boat became almost vertical at the limit of its swing.

'Hey, listen! There's that song again,' Ronnie shouted. The harmonious wailing of a new duo called the Everly Brothers came to them through the merry din.

'Bye Bye Love...'

'Yeah, they're playin' deadly ones. D'yeh know what, if I had loadsa money I'd buy every one of them.'

The night fairly crackled with Rock 'n 'Roll excitement.

'She's Got It', screamed Little Richard. 'The Girl Can't Help It'.

Paul Anka pleaded with Diana.

'Don't You Rock Me, Daddio', warned Lonnie Donegan.

And every second record seemed to be by the man they were already calling the King. With numbers like 'Too Much', 'Teddy Bear', the irresistible 'All Shook Up' and his latest hit, 'Paralysed', he rocked them on the roundabouts, the chair-o-planes, the whip and the octopus, and away across the railway tracks people strolling on the promenade sang along as the sound wafted past them and on out over the black rolling waves.

'Half past eight, son,' a deep Scottish voice answered his query as to the hour of the night.

Already! Flip it anyway. That was quick. He would have to run all the way to get home by nine, which was as late as he was allowed stay out. It wasn't unheard of for Ma to be waiting at the end of the lane brandishing the leather strap should he or Val attempt to stretch this limit.

He took his last two pennies from the pocket of his first pair of longers. The only thing available at the carnival for tuppence was a ticket at the huge circular raffle stall, piled high with all manner of gaudy prizes. The great bank of numbered squares rotated like a giant radar scanner, a light hopping from number to number as it turned.

It came to a stop and his number remained lit up.

For his prize he chose a pair of toy binoculars which he turned and trained on the nearby International Hotel. Realizing he could see that noble edifice better with the naked eye he asked one of the ticket sellers if he would give him something else instead.

'I will an' me bollix,' he said kindly.

Louser.

There were several ticket sellers moving around inside the circle and when a different one approached him Ray chanced his arm again.

'Eh, mister, can I change these for somethin' else?'

'What d'yeh want then, hurry, yeh'll be gettin' me gev out to.'

He had spotted a big holy picture that Ma would like, and pointed to it.

'Righty-o, sure yeh couldn't go wrong with the like a' that.'

'It's for me Mammy,' he said quickly.

He had to screwge in between two fat oul'ones to take the picture from the man.

'Yer a great boy! Isn't it grand to see the bitta religion in the young, Maggie,' one of them remarked. 'That'll bring yer Mammy good luck. Maybe she'll win the Fifty on Monday.'

Yeah, an' the cat'll bring in an elephant be the scruff idda neck.

The picture was divided in three; Jesus on one side, Mary on the other, the pair of them separated by a mirror, so that by the simple act of gawking in the mirror you placed yourself in company of the highest order.

It hung for many years above the mantelpiece, where the red glow from the little paraffin lamp highlighted the bleeding heart of Jesus. Ma never let that lamp go out and they called it the Little Lamp to distinguish it from the big one in her bedroom.

Bray had lost its lighthouse during a freak summer storm. It had broken away from the end of the pier and hung suspended at a crazy angle for a whole day while the sea did its mighty best to send it to the bottom. Dad, Val and Ray were among the sodden crowd who stood on the shore and braved the tempest hoping to see the final plunge. The stricken tower held on stubbornly and in the end the intrepid trio squelched home to Ma who asked were they all in it or what, to be standin' out in the elements an' it lashin' out of the heavens, that there were people locked up in Grangegorman for less.

'Ah, whist, will yeh,' said Dad as he shook the rain from his hat. 'Sure there's not a cormer on us. It's a nice warm rain, an' we're not sugarbabbies.'

In October things took a turn for the better when Dad got a new job. A big old house on the back road called Ardmore was to become home to some film studios, and Dad had put his name down for a job as gardener, not knowing if they would even need such a thing.

'Sure they might have somethin' else I could do. E'er a job is better than ne'er a one.'

When word came to the house that he was to attend for an interview right away he wasn't at home.

'Quick,' Ma said, 'take my bike an' get down to Bray as fast as yeh can. Tell yer father to go over to Ardmore immediately, an' God grant he gets the job.'

Ray was delighted with the spin. He pedalled furiously up and down the hills, turning off Main Street and down Novara Avenue to a house called Beechfield where Dad had procured a day's work. He was raking the gravel in front of the house when Ray arrived with the news, and they cycled up Herbert Road to Ardmore together.

Ray waited at the gate and when he saw Dad coming back from the interview with a grin on him that you could post a letter through, he knew he had got the job.

'Well, thanks bitta God for that anyway!' he puffed happily as they rolled along Darby's Lane. 'Yer Mammy'll be charmed, God love her. The oul' bills is gone to hell altogether.'

Ma was charmed all right, and still in such good form at Halloween that she dressed up and went around the cottages baffling and amusing all the neighbours by refusing to say a word when asked in. She would just sit there making the sort of noises that might be expected to come from a cat in the process of being throttled. The oul' ones made wild guesses as to her identity, all of them thinking it had to be one of the older children.

Mrs. Hughes brought her face close to the witches mask and squinted at the mischievous eyes behind it.

'I think it's one of them Kavanagh young-ones from up the Buildin's,' she said, and reached as if to whip the mask from Ma's face.

'Mrkngiaowrl!'

Mrs. Hughes jumped back in alarm as Ma made a flying lep out of the chair at her.

'Sacred Heart a' Jesus!'

Ma settled back in silence, her eyes glaring at her startled neighbour, and every time the unfortunate lady made a move or attempted to speak she would give another wild snarling bucklep.

'The divil roast yeh for a mad hoor, whoever yeh are,'

Val and Ray stood by in their own costumes, almost choking with laughter as Ma stole their thunder. Ray was a bit windy that Mrs. Hughes might take a swipe at Ma if she kept up her antics. She could easily have flattened Ma, but having no idea who might be behind the mask, she held off

Back home Ma collapsed into the armchair and lifted the mask to reveal the wonderful heart-warming sight of tears streaming down her laughing face.

'Oh, good stick!' she gasped. 'I haven't had such a good laugh since the bucket was a thimble. Did yiz see the look on oul' Hughes's face? She didn't know what the hell to make a' me. Yeh should've dressed up an' come out yourself, Jem.'

'Ay,' Dad said, 'an' have them all thinkin' I'm as quare as the rest of yiz. No fear!'

'Ah, go an' scrape, yeh oul' stick-in-the-mud,' she chuckled, throwing the mask at him.

'It's a good job yeh didn't take that thing off while yeh were out or yidda been arrested.'

'Huh! D'yeh hear Handsome Harry talkin' an' him with a bake on him like a feckin' parrot. Pretty polly! Pretty Polly!' she chirped.

It was a moment to cherish; to store away safely, to be unwrapped and savoured in less cheerful times.

Now as he spread the year's dead leaves on the floor of the hen-shed he felt a sadness that was only partially tempered by anticipation of the unknown new excitements the following year might bring.

He stood in the doorway of the shed in the twilight, the hens rustling about behind him. The light came on in the kitchen and he thought how peaceful it all looked. For a long time he stayed watching the shadows come and go across the flowery-patterned curtains, and as darkness fell on Ballywaltrim the night was so still that, as Dad might remark, you could hear the snails grazin'.

The hens, quiet now except for the odd low cluck, settled on their perches for the night.

CHAPTER TWENTY

'Right! That's it then. I'm goin' an' yiz'll never see me in this cursed kip again. I warned yiz. Time outa bloody mind I warned yiz, an' now yiz've driven me to it. I'm leavin', an' the divil fucked ever I'll darken the door again.'

The back door opened and slammed.

'Ah, God help us,' Dad murmured.

Before the echo of the slamming door had faded Ray was out of bed. He had been following the one-sided row as it progressed from one subject to another, almost always coming back to Dad's alleged incompetence as a father.

'Daddy...'

'Japers, son, we didn't mean to wake yeh up. Now don't worry, yer Mammy'll come back all right. She...'

'Will I folly her, Daddy?'

'Would yeh, son? Just to be on the safe side. She'll prob'ly just have a walk to make her feel better. A bit of a dander when yer upset works wonders.'

Ray was not so sure. Ma had often threatened to feck off out of it before, but had never actually crossed the door. He looked at the clock. Eleven twenty, and it was freezing out there.

He pulled on his clothes, turning up the collar of the heavy overcoat Ma had got for him on tick from Sloan's at Christmas. Running as far as Jones's gate he caught sight of her slight figure as she passed under the bottom light. She was wearing her 'furbackers', the big warm gloves that everybody in the house liked to borrow. The icy breeze nearly froze the tears on his cheeks.

Oh Mammy, please ... we love you.

She turned towards Bray. He snuffled and jumped into Butler's field, running down to the end and waiting inside the hedge until he heard her footsteps passing on the main road.

The night was black but he was able to follow the clicking of her heels as she turned into the even inkier blackness between the high hedges of Boghall Road. She stepped briskly along for about a quarter of a mile and as she approached the first of the Boghall Cottages a dog - a big dog if its bulk bore any relation to its bark - started up a savage howling.

Ma's footsteps faltered, then moved forward hesitantly. He was terrified. What if it attacked her? What could he do? It soon became apparent, when the dog failed to come charging onto the road, that it must be tied up in one of the front gardens.

She walked on, getting back into her stride, and the dog continued its howling, the sound of its paws thumping and tearing at the ground in its efforts to get free even more chilling than the ferocious barking. He prayed it was on a good strong leash.

She turned off left into the Soldier's Road. Good. It would take her back to the main road nearer Bray. When she came to the junction she stopped and stood in the glow of the same lamp Ray had quaked under waiting for the lights of a car.

Ma wasn't waiting for a car. She wasn't afraid of the dark. At least she said she wasn't. Anyway it was nearly midnight and highly unlikely that any cars would be coming along.

She was wearing her white coat. He remembered the joy he used to feel on Sundays in the hospital when he would spot that coat emerging from the passageway onto the veranda. Nearly four years ago now, and it wasn't so white anymore, but still her 'good' coat.

He pondered the awful prospect of never seeing her again. There would be no more ructions, of course, but that didn't even begin to make the idea of life without her thinkable.

'She doesn't be well in herself, God love her,' Dad would say, 'but she loves yiz just the same.'

And she did. Of course she loved them. That was why, in spite of all the rows and uproars, home without Ma was an appalling notion. For a start, Dad couldn't make a decent pot of porridge to save his life. Those yukky slimy lumps if he had to do breakfast duty! Woeful tack.

And didn't she always look after them when they were sick? Coming in every night before going to bed to put Holy Water on their feverish foreheads, or, if they were really poorly, taking out the little bottle of Lourdes water with the green scum on it and letting them swig a sup of it.

Even the neighbours sent for Ma if somebody was ill, and so many of them made a rapid recovery following a sprinkle from her little bottle that she must have posed a threat to the local dispensary doctor. She would sit and nurse seriously ill people and was highly regarded for taking on things nobody else would have the stomach for. Dad put her minor miracles down to the fact that once Ma assured a person that he or she would recover, 'the poor craythur wouldn't darr kick the bucket'.

So, he surmised, if she gladly performed all of these charitable deeds, Ma couldn't be anything less than a good woman, and that being the case she would hardly be likely to just feck off and leave her own family. He felt a touch of optimism.

But what was wrong? Why all those crushing, dispiriting tempers? What were Dad and the rest of the family doing that was so terribly wicked? And why did she expect them to be perfect while at the same time endlessly drumming it into them that they were anything but, and never would be?

He stamped his feet and blew into his hands. It was no night to be standing about, but at least it was dry. He had pushed himself well into the brambles, his head stuck out watching.

Ma was walking back and forth from one side of the road to the other, whether to keep warm or because she couldn't make up her mind which way to go he couldn't guess.

Please go up Fairy Hill. Please!

She continued her pacing, showing no inclination to move on from the crossroads. All the everyday taken-for-granted things she did for them passed before his mind's eye like a series of snippets from a long, sad film.

Ma down on her knees scrubbing the grey concrete floor;

Ma sitting up until all hours making clothes for her kids from other peoples' cast-offs;

Ma mixing the big pot of potato skins and Layer's Mash for the hens in the hope that it might encourage the chook-chooks to earn their keep;

Ma struggling to push the pram up the hills from Bray with several whinging gets hanging out of it;

Ma scribbling the little things she thought for a moment she could afford from the shopping list, and Ma striving endlessly in the hopeless battle of the bills.

Even with Dad working at Ardmore, six pounds a week for a family of eight took some stretching, and she was as far now from her nice bit of carpet as she had ever been.

He felt so helplessly sorry for her. It was all so unfair.

He thought of the truly shocking state she had been in the day she had gone to the dentist and come home without a single tooth in her head. He had seen the tears of pain dripping onto the black range as she got stuck into cleaning it the moment she got home. For days she couldn't speak, her face a woeful picture.

But there was no rest.

Anyone else in the house could be ill and go to bed. Ma could only be ill.

He pictured the little girl playing all those years ago in the Phoenix Park and his eyes filled.

'I used to love swingin' under an' over the iron railin's in the People's Gardens,' she had told him one time, misty-eyed. 'An' Kitty an' Molly goin' mad lookin' at me 'cause they couldn't master it at all. Green they were! I must take yiz up there sometime. It's lovely in the summer when all the flowers are out.'

And he tried to imagine the terror and incomprehension of little Lulu James cowering under her bed in a futile attempt at avoiding the cruel blows of the sweeping brush wielded by her drunken father. It was like Dad said, she couldn't help it, the tempers and that; it was the way life and long years of soul-destroying poverty had made her.

He wanted to run up to her under that lonely streetlight and hug her.

There now, Ma. There now.

On top of all her own woes she worried about Kitty and Noel, that 'lazy pair a' lunatics' in Windgates. She and Dad had gone there one day offering to clean the place up a bit and Noel had chased them back out the gate, threatening that if they showed their faces out there again he would brain them with the hatchet, a much favoured implement, it would appear, in Ma's family for such work. Ma, of course, never a paragon of diplomacy, had probably gone in with guns blazing, informing them in no uncertain language of her opinion of folk who lived in such squalor.

He was almost too cold to move when she finally started up the hill.

Oh, thank you, God, thank you!

The brambles were reluctant to let him go, pulling and plucking at his coat as he stepped from his hiding place to follow her. A white frost glittered on the road beneath the light at the crossroads. To get past her and home first, he climbed the gate into Tom Costello's field and ran down the other side of the hill inside the hedgerow. The frozen grass crunched under his feet like spilled cornflakes. Near the end of the field, just as he was about to climb out at Boghall corner, his right foot sank into a soft, deep and very cold cow-dung.

Obviously the frost wasn't quite as severe as it seemed.

He frantically wiped as much as he could off but couldn't afford to delay; he could hear Ma's footfalls approaching. Safely into Butler's field with a minute or two to spare, he dragged his leg this way and that in the grass until his shoe and trousers were soaked but clean.

'She's coming back!' he gasped as he burst in the back door, whipped his coat off and vanished into the bedroom. He couldn't leave his wet shoe at the range to dry; she would be sure to twig something. A thankful shudder ran through him as he slipped between the sheets. Ma came in less than a minute behind him and went straight to bed without saying a word. For an hour or more he could hear the soft pop-pop of Dad puffing his pipe, and he thought it was the most peaceful sound in the world.

'Hey, you out there! It's half shaggin' one in the mornin'. Are yeh goin' to sit hatchin' the fire like a feckin' leprechaun all night?

Dad heaved a long sigh of resignation.

'Will yeh lave me alone, or have yeh ne'er a bitta nature in yeh at all?'

There was a choked pleading in his voice.

'That's your answer to everything, isn't it? Lave me alone. Lave me a-fuckinwell-lone.'

Ray heard him tapping the ashes from his pipe on the range.

The kitchen light went out.

CHAPTER TWENTY-ONE

In the sloping field between Ballywaltrim Lane and the new garage at Hollybrook some boys and girls from the cottages were enjoying the unexpected bonus of a snowfall on All Fools Day.

The homemade sleighs hissed, bumped and overturned amid shouts and squeals of delight. It wasn't as good a field for the job as the Tower Field in Hodson's, but all the sleighs had been brought down from there at what was reckoned to be the end of winter, and it was not deemed worth the long haul back up for a late snowfall which in all probability would vanish overnight.

Ray was pulling his sleigh up the slope when he heard his name called and turned to see Eamonn Dunne beckoning him from the road. Eamonn, who had been in St. Cronan's with him and lived in Wolfe Tone Square, was now an apprentice mechanic at the garage.

He plodded up to the wall.

'Good Eamonn.'

Good. D'yeh want a job?'

'Where?'

'In the garage.'

'What doin'?'

'On the petrol pumps. It's a cinch. If yeh want it come up an' see Paddy Farrell.'

In the warmth of the tiny office-cum-shop at the garage Paddy said he would pay him fifteen shillings a week and he would have to work every second Sunday. Ray was hesitant. It would mean working until ten o'clock on weeknights. It seemed like an awful lot of hours for fifteen bob, and anyway at the Tech he was actually enjoying school for the first time.

To his surprise, when he told Ma about the offer she jumped at the idea.

'Go back up there an' tell him yeh'll take it. A job's a job an' yeh can't afford to be turnin' down opportunities. There's many a poor wretch on the dole that'd be charmed with a grand easy job like that.'

He afterwards realized that Ma had reasons other than the obvious economic ones for wishing him to have the job.

There had been a short while back a religious retreat at the Tech, and at one of the lectures given to a mixed group in the gym the visiting priest kept referring to 'The Process'. Men and women had to go through 'The Process' in order to produce babies. He made it sound like some tedious duty, a necessary evil performed only because God, in a careless moment, had unwittingly allowed a piece of filth to fall into his plan for the world.

No reference whatsoever was made concerning what exactly this 'Process' was or what it entailed, or even if it had a name other than 'The Process', but scattered sniggers suggested that any further elaboration on the subject was unnecessary for some at least, and Ray himself had probably witnessed more of 'The Process' than the reverend gentleman was ever likely to, given his chosen walk in life.

The lecture did, however, arouse the curiosity of four of those present to the extent that they got up to some carry on that very afternoon which resulted in their being expelled from the school the following day.

When news of the expulsions broke, wild rumours abounded among the students, while teachers and parents maintained a tight-lipped silence on the subject.

'Don't you be mindin' them young-ones down in that Tech now, d'yeh hear me?' was Ma's only comment, there being little more she could say without admitting to the existence of 'The Process'.

Could she have read his mind she would have seen that he would most certainly 'mind those young-ones' if he could only overcome his shyness, but he was increasingly feeling that he somehow wasn't good enough; that going out with pretty girls was something other lads did, and the idea that a girl could actually like him had gradually become a ridiculous notion outside the realm of reality. He could think of nothing in particular that had occurred to make him feel this way; he just did, and it caused him to build imaginary snubs into monumental rejections.

He never laid eyes on the four unlucky lechers again, but the story of what had allegedly taken place filtered back over the following days. The two young ladies had apparently agreed to go into a field on the outskirts of Bray with the boys and had there generously consented to the removal of their knickers, at the same time pointing out that this was the only item of clothing they wished to divest themselves of. Had the pair of Romeos been satisfied with this kind offer they might never have come to grief, but, their appetites whetted, they became greedy and after much cajoling managed to persuade the lassies to disrobe completely.

They then embarked on the course of action that was to be their downfall. They decided, in case the girls should get any ideas about cutting short this agreeable adventure, to hide their clothing out of reach up a nearby tree, so that when the local farmer arrived on the happy scene they were caught literally with their pants down, unable to make a run for it.

Many and varied were the conjectures put forward among the students as to the fate likely to befall the two unfortunate girls.

They would have babies.

They would never be able to have babies.

They would be locked up in a home forever.

They would have to be washed in a bath of holy water by a bishop.

They would be goin' mad for it' from now on.

They would go to hell and the divil would pay particular attention to their private parts with his red-hot poker.

There was no talk of punishment for the boys.

Ma would inevitably have got wind of the escapade and grave doubts would have assailed her about the kind of influences that were abroad in the Tech and their possible corrupting effects on her son, so the timely turning up of a job for him would have been like the answer to a prayer. She could whip him out of that den of iniquity without the awkwardness of having to explain.

And so he found himself pumping petrol at Hollybrook Garage. He quite enjoyed getting to know the various makes of car and meeting a wide variety of new people.

Four and ninepence a gallon.

Some well-off drivers would say to make it the pound's worth. More than four gallons.

A full quid!

His whole weeks wages and one third on top of it. Just for petrol!

You could buy three records for that, with enough left over for a visit to the picture house, ice cream, chips and the bus home.

Paddy Farrell was a rather rotund, jolly man, given to moving people out of his way with a friendly bump of his big belly. He drove a Ford Zephyr Six and on Sunday mornings picked Ray up at the end of the Lane and took him to nine o'clock Mass in Bray before opening the garage.

Chauffeur-driven! ZU 5315.

Heaters! Warm as a thrush's nest.

Oil was sold from crates on the forecourt in one and two-pint bottles and Paddy told him to save the foil bottle-caps in as good condition as possible, then in the tiny room off the office during slack periods they would refill the bottles with oil from a barrel, re-sealing the caps by pressing the edges under the rim of the neck with the back of a knife.

In the dark evenings some of the local men would call in for a chat around the battered old paraffin heater in the office. Mick Ryan, father of young Mary of the Hilly Field, would come down the stony Giltspur Lane carrying his wireless battery to be recharged. No electricity at Hollybrook Back Lodge yet.

'Oh jeez, 'tis cold, Ray!' he would puff, rubbing his hands together briskly over the heater.

Johnny Hughes from the Buildings, Frankie O'Farrell from Ballywaltrim House, Willie Griffin, Ray's metalwork teacher at the Tech, crossed the road from the lodge at the main gate of Hollybrook House, and Tommy Mustard coaxed his ancient blue Ford Popular from O'Byrne Road.

Often, to Ray's dismay, the conversation would turn to tales of strange and ghostly happenings; not the sort of stories a lad needs to hear when he has a lonely quarter-mile walk ahead of him boasting a haunted house between himself and home.

' 'Tis true, Ray, 'tis true!' Mick Ryan would assure him in his warm Tipperary brogue, his eyes twinkling with mischief.

He was always grateful to see Tommy Mustard arriving, because on the nights Tommy was there he would get a lift to the end of the lane. Tommy's car was a sight to behold. The rear suspension had gone on one side causing it to sit down on one corner, as Tommy put it, 'draggin' its arse along the road', and about two-thirds of the windscreen was clouded by an oily stain so that Tommy had to lean sideways as he drove in order to see out through the clear bit.

Sometimes on a Sunday afternoon the delectable Daisy Dunne dropped in. He guessed Daisy was about to leave her teens while he was barely into his. In the close confines of the office he found her overwhelmingly attractive

213

and he was desperately afraid that something very embarrassing might happen.

She seemed to take delight in shocking the men with her outrageous jokes and comments, most of which he didn't understand.

Like that day with the lemonade.

Somebody made her laugh while she was having a swig from a large bottle, causing her to spill some down inside her blouse. She said she preferred her own lubricant to that of Taylor Keith, whatever the hell that meant. She shook herself as she spoke making her breasts wobble delightfully.

The men laughed and made appreciative noises, then somebody cautioned her that there was a young-lad present, and the young-lad fervently wished that person would mind his own bloomin' business.

Her skirts were always body hugging, so that her nylons sang as her thighs brushed against each other when she walked, and oh, holy divine God, wasn't that the loveliest, most magical music ever to bless the human ear.

He thought about Daisy a lot, and each time he did so he wound up with another mortal sin on his soul. It was useless to resist the monstrous temptation. Guilt and the dreadful fear of hell melted before its majesty. Then something happened that put a stop to his gallop for a while. One moment he had been in high heaven, the next in terror of his life.

Something...some liquidy stuff had...

Oh no! Oh jeezmammy what's that? I've got something terrible. I'll die! I swear, God, I swear! Never again. Ever!

214

A few days later he was fighting a losing battle. In despair he tried to banish the impure thoughts from his mind by thinking about the hideous disease he had probably given himself and would doubtless exacerbate by indulging in that black sin again. He thought of Ma catching him and dragging him off to the priest.

All to no avail. He was trying to stop a steamroller with a straw. As he surrendered he had the neck to ask God to please not let there be any alarming outcome this time.

There was. Even more than the last time.

That was it then. He was done for. A goner.

He remembered with horror poor Joe at the hospital, and the quare thing that had happened as the nurse tried to shave him. This must be the same affliction. How long before he was stricken like Joe? He lived on the edge of panic for weeks. There was nobody he could confide in. Telling Ma was out of the question. Better just to die and let them discover the cause afterwards. That would at least save him the shame of it.

It would be straight to hell for him, of course, and no need to feel embarrassed before the Divil, who would have heard it all before.

Or would he?

He sneaked into Ma's bedroom one day and sprinkled a few drops of Lourdes water on the cause of his appalling predicament, and as time passed with no sign of the expected deterioration in his health his faith in the powers of Holy Water soared. He was going to live. He felt like celebrating.

Just this once.

After this last time he would give it up forever.

CHAPTER TWENTY-TWO

The five bob he kept for himself out of his wages meant he could buy the occasional record, and Irene Murray, the pretty assistant in Kent & Byrne's shop on Quinsboro' Road, kept aside a copy of each new Presley single for him as it became available, writing his name on the brown paper sleeve.

It was midsummer and once again the seafront was the place to be. Down by the railway bridge the old lady sold her boxes of matches while nearby the blind accordionist threw his head from side to side in time with his music, both of them as much a part of Bray in the holiday season as Punch and Judy. On the esplanade you had to be on the ball early to find a space to sit on the grass.

By now most of the old crooners and bands had disappeared from the jukeboxes and many new voices had joined the early pioneers of Rock 'n' Roll to help send them on their way.

Names like Jerry Lee Lewis, Buddy Holly, Ricky Nelson and Bobby Darin now made their presence felt, and the songs of 1958 bore some of the most outlandish titles in musical history: 'Bony Moronie', 'Purple People Eater', 'Great Balls of Fire', 'Bird Dog', 'Rave on', 'Yacketty Yak', 'Splish Splash', 'Good Golly Miss Molly,' and Connie Francis, the first female Rock 'n' Roller, had the teens bopping to 'Stupid Cupid'.

Presley fans celebrated as their hero's 'Jailhouse Rock' became the first song ever to enter the charts at number one, and Elvis introduced a new word to their vocabulary, the word for 'It' or The Process, when he stood behind Judy Tyler in the film 'Jailhouse Rock' and mumbled: 'Hmm, you look sexy tonight!

The girls who thronged the beach now seemed almost unbearably beautiful, and as their attractiveness increased so too did his conviction that for him they were a hopelessly unattainable dream. It was a joke even to think of the likes of him ever being able to communicate intelligibly with such beauty.

Not even when they approached him, like that nice-looking English girl who had come over to him one day in Dawson's Amusements, brushing against him tantalizingly as they stood by the jukebox, she singing 'All I Have to do is Dream' along with the Everly Brothers.

He was paralysed.

'Play the flip side,' she requested. 'Play Claudette, it's a cool rocker.'

He strove to break out of his stricken state, to dive in and enthusiastically discuss with her the merits or otherwise of the various records stacked before them in their gaudy glass palace. He knew every one of them, B-sides and all, but surely the fact that the girl spoke to him at all could only mean one thing - that she was out to have some kind of laugh at his expense. His mind absolutely disallowed the possibility of any other motive.

He stood for a few seconds like one o' clock half struck, then gave her a stupid grin, gulped awkwardly and walked away, face burning and tears of rage threatening to burst forth at any moment.

A soothing breeze came in off the Irish Sea as he walked onto the promenade. He stopped and bent his head so that his brow touched the cool sugar-stick-twist iron railing, and closed his eyes.

Thousands of voices, most of them laughing it seemed, filled the balmy air around him. Squeals of delight as waves washed over toddlers; the splish splash of Pedalo boats just off shore; musical chiming from the Guinness clock as it entertained another gathering with its clever moving figures; the distant whirr and grind of the aerial chairlift as it carried excited holidaymakers up the side of Bray Head to the Eagle's Nest, and the faint sound of Irish dance music drifting along the esplanade from the bandstand.

The whole world seemed to be having a grand time except for himself and the youngster whose whining for an ice lollipop turned abruptly to a surprised yelp as his long-suffering mother's patience ran out.

To hell with it! He wasn't fifteen yet. He would think it out and solve it. Identify and tear out by the roots whatever it was that caused him to feel the way he did.

The black tooth didn't help. He had acquired it through the lick of a hurley stick to the mouth while playing rounders in Butler's field. The tooth had cracked across and the lower half had quickly become discoloured, leaving him with a great reluctance to smile, and a tendency to greet the world with a face as long as a fortnight. On the odd occasion when, caught off guard, a grin slipped through and lit his features, it was swiftly extinguished as he realized his mistake and clamped his lips together like the curtain suddenly descending on a play in mid-act.

He wouldn't go near a dentist with it in spite of Ma's constant entreaties to do so. Not that he feared the dentist. In Primary School it had been a much-utilized dodge among

219

the boys to have a tooth pulled just to get some time off. All you needed was a molar that exhibited even the slightest sign of decay and you were sent down to the clinic at around ten o'clock. The blood spilled was considered a small price to pay for having the rest of the day free. No. What bothered him was the prospect of going around with a front tooth missing.

A black tooth was one thing, a black hole quite another.

And it would gape there for many a long month until his gum was hard enough for him to be fitted with a false tombstone stuck on the end of one of those disgusting palate things that Ma's teeth were on. It would surely spell the end of his secretly harboured hopes of someday becoming a singer. How the hell could a lad sing with a great chunk of delph wedged in his gob?

Somebody told him he could have it capped, but it was impossibly expensive and, being considered a luxury, was not available on the National Health. For the time being, until fortune smiled on him, he would just have to grin, or rather refrain from grinning, and bear it.

Dodging prams, go-cars, dogs and kids that made sudden darts in all directions, he made his way along the prom and crossed over to the Fun Palace where he pushed some coins into the slot and, selecting the loudest, wildest records on the jukebox, allowed Little Richard to scream out his frustration for him.

CHAPTER TWENTY-THREE

Ma had often voiced her opinion that the boys, useless as they were for anything better, would wind up 'pushing bloody messenger-boys' bikes', and before the end of 1958 Ray had obligingly made her prophecy come true. The job, at Hayes, Conyngham and Robinson's chemist's shop on Quinsboro' Road, offered one pound ten shillings a week and a one hundred per cent increase was not to be sneezed at, so pride took a back seat.

Mr. Couse, the shop manager, was an impeccably neat man with a shiny bald head and the bearing of a soldier. He appeared to stand an inch or two beyond upright, shoulders pulled back so far that he always looked in danger of falling over backwards.

'Yid think he was after swallyin' a fuckin' crowbar', the messenger boy from Lipton's across the road remarked.

'Take your hands out of your pockets when you speak to me, sonny!' he had ordered when Ray approached him about the job.

Ray obeyed sheepishly. It was not that he was lacking in good manners or respect, but on a freezing November afternoon with a wind coming up from the sea that would skin an Eskimo's cat, pockets were the places for hands while being interviewed outside a shop door.

That winter, spent pushing an unwieldy bike with its big basket around Bray, was a bone-chilling experience.

He nearly froze to death on that lousy bike.

His fingers froze around the bare steel handlebars no matter how he tried to keep the circulation going. Worst of all was the big scales for weighing new babies. When a family added another member to the community the awkward scales would be loaded into the basket, making the bike so ridiculously top-heavy that it took all his ingenuity and strength just to hold the thing upright, never mind mount and cycle it. And of course most of the new arrivals were being born to residents of the furthest-flung new estates like Raheen Park, halfway up feckin' Bray Head.

As he battled through driving sleet that felt as if it were tearing holes in his face he cursed himself for a gobshite for leaving the cosy warmth of the little office at the garage.

'Down for the day be the look of it!' Somebody shouted cheerfully.

Ah, go an' shite!

Between deliveries he waited in the cellar beneath the shop. Where the cellar extended out under the pavement it was roofed with small squares of thick glass through which he passed the time looking up the skirts of distorted ladies as they moved up and down the road, some of them obligingly stopping for a look in the shop window.

On Christmas Eve, after he had completed his last marrow-numbing trip for that day, Mr. Couse came down to the cellar and handed him his wages. He then proceeded to count out five florins into his hand, which was now throbbing in agony as life returned to it.

'There you are, sonny! Ten shillings for your Christmas box. Out of my own pocket, mind you. Happy Christmas now, sonny!'

He stuck his hand out and Ray took it. Three firm shakes and Mr. Couse stood back, clicked his shoes together, spun on his heel and marched back up the stairs to the shop, having performed the little ceremony with all the stiff-lipped precision of a general pinning a medal on a private.

Ray studied the pile of silver in his hand appreciatively. It was the biggest Christmas box he had ever received, and taken together with the odd bob and tanner he had been given during the day by customers it brought his collection, not counting his wages, to just over a pound.

He bounded up the stairs and out of the shop, calling 'Happy Christmas' to Paddy Maguire and Eileen King, the two assistants, as he went, and crossed the sleet-lashed Quinsboro' Road to Kent and Byrne's from whence he emerged shortly with a copy of Elvis' Christmas Album under his oxter.

He could now play LPs at home, having wheedled Ma into buying a radiogram on the Kathleen Mavourneen and promising to share the repayments. She referred to it as 'that infernal box' and swore its sound quality wasn't a patch on that of the old gramophone, which was once again sadly silent after its startling but short-lived reawakening.

Also short-lived was his sojourn at Hayes, Conyngham and Robinson's. In February he applied for and got a job as helper on a Dargle and Bray Laundry van, which brought his wages up another eight shillings, and held prospects, if a lad stuck it out, of getting one's own van and laundry round at the age of eighteen.

The extra few bob meant that most Sundays now they could afford an ox heart to roast in the oven, packed with Ma's delicious stuffing, sheer luxury after years of spuds and cabbage, spuds and peas, spuds and Chef sauce or just spuds, the monotony only broken now and then by a sheep's head or a pig's cheek.

A sheep's head on the dinner table is a singularly grisly sight and one that could hardly be regarded as being conducive to a hearty appetite, but hunger is good sauce, Ma would remark, and nobody turned a nose up at it. The brains were of a crunchy texture and tasteless, crumbling in the mouth like boiled cauliflower. Nobody mourned the passing of this delicacy from the menu at number fifteen.

Dad was happy at his work in the film studios and before long was 'promoted' from the garden to the props department. He delighted in regaling them with stories of film stars he met and was really up in the boughs when James Cagney, one of his own boyhood heroes, came to Ardmore to film 'Shake Hands With The Devil'.

'Did yeh meet him, Daddy?'

'Did I what? Sure didn't he have a cuppa tay with me in the prop shed!'

There wasn't much Dad could be told about the early days of cinema. As a young man he had worked in the projection room of the now long defunct McDermott's Picture House which was housed in the once-beautiful nineteenth century Turkish Baths building on Quinsboro' Road, now semi-derelict, but with its tall minarets still standing out against the sky making it the most distinctive structure in the town.

He was proud of the family's deep roots in Bray.

'Our people have been here since oul' God's time, fishermen they were before there was e'er a town a' Bray at all, an' many a one a'them was drowned long ago when there

224

was ne'er a harbour. An' didn't one a' them mind that famous writer fella that lived near where the harbour is now. She looked after him an' he on'y a child. Jack told me the same chap put our name on some fella in his books on'y he spelled it wrong. Imagine that now, an' he a writer!'

One dark evening Dad was unusually late getting home and Ma, becoming anxious, went outside to see if there was any sign of him. She was shocked to find him lying at the side of the Lane near the gate, sobbing in a most disconcerting manner that he had been hit by a car, and that the louser had driven on without checking to see if he was dead or alive.

'Jesus mercy, Jimmy, where are yeh hurt?'

She managed to get him to his feet and walk him inside to the bedroom where he lay, still crying and insisting he had been run over. Ray came in to find Ma in an awful state.

'Yeh better run back along the road an' see if yeh can find the bike,' she said. 'We'll know by it if he was really knocked down.'

There was no sign of it in the Lane or on Killarney Road, nor was it anywhere along Darby's Lane, and when he got out onto the back road he stepped carefully in the pitch darkness towards Ardmore, feeling ahead with his foot for fear of stumbling over it.

He saw a faint light some distance down the road.

Good. I'll ask whoever it is if they saw a bike lying about.

The light, when he came up to it, turned out to be Dad's own, still in place on the bike and shining weakly

225

through the brambles into which it had fallen. He extricated it from the thorny hedgerow and, finding no evidence of a collision, cycled home to tell Ma the good news.

Dad was still wailing in the front room when he got back, and Ma was at her wits end.

'Sacred heart a' God, will yeh listen to him. Wouldn't that put the heart crossways in yeh. Go down quick an' ask Mrs. Healy to come up for a minute.'

For once it was Ma who needed a neighbour.

Mrs. Healy took one look at Dad whinging to himself in the bed and laughed, assuring Ma that he was nothing more than stotious drunk.

'Well bad cess to him anyway, givin' me a land like that! Imagine gettin' himself into a state like that with curse a' God drink.'

Dad's story the next day was that a party had been given at the Royal Hotel to celebrate the completion of the latest Ardmore film, 'A Terrible Beauty', which starred Robert Mitchum and a new young Irish actor called Richard Harris. The party was intended for the stars and bigwigs of the film industry only, so the ordinary studio workers arranged a bit of a hooley of their own in one of the studio buildings. For some unknown reason Mitchum and Harris deserted the lavish spread and exalted company in the Royal and turned up at Ardmore to join the prop-men and carpenters. They sang and told yarns while the drink flowed as freely as the Dargle in the valley below.

For Dad, who had never in his life downed more than a bottle or two of stout on special occasions, it could only mean disaster. By the time it was over he was incapable

226

of seeing a hole in a forty-foot ladder. As for his alleged encounter with a car, he had no recollection of even mentioning such a thing.

There wasn't a cormer on him.

Ray's black tooth now began to disintegrate and he resorted to buying little white sticks of rubbery stuff at the chemist's, which he melted down and stuffed into the cavities. This temporary filling contrasted so sharply with the tooth that his smile was even more outlandish than before, and worse still, it turned from brilliant white to disgusting yellow in a matter of weeks, so that he regularly had to set about the nauseating task of renewing it.

On his first visit to the pictures alone at night he came out of the Royal into a different world than that from which he had come in. It was snowing heavily and the roads, even the Main Street, were already thickly blanketed. Snowballs whizzed into the midst of the emerging crowd, flung by a group of laughing gets on the opposite side of the road.

'Get to hell outa that, yiz shower a' bowsies!' one of the victims yelled, and a few men made a run at the ambushers, who went skittering and falling down Quinsboro' Road, shouting abuse.

'If I get a hold a' yiz, I'll lave yiz that yer oul' ones won't know yiz from a hape a'shite!'

'Nyeh nyeh nyeh nyeh nyeh! Hey, how's yer belly for spots, yeh oul' gobdaw?'

Up the Main Street some people waited outside McCarthy's for the Wicklow bus, looking very much like a Dickensian group on a Christmas card with their mufflers, gloves, turned up collars, turned down hats, and backs hunched against the flurries of snow.

It had been his intention to get the bus home himself, but a walk home through a blizzard was not an experience to be foregone for the sake of comfort. The film had been a trap and cut to ribbons, but this would more than make up for it.

He didn't meet another soul on the way. In the dip at Patchwork the little river in the Scotch Glen below the road sounded louder than usual in the snow-hushed night. He leaned over the low parapet but all he could see were snowflakes vanishing down into the blackness. Many times he and his friends had tempted fate by walking that low wall on the way home from school. Ma would have had a seizure if she had seen them.

The road ahead held no terrors for him tonight as he left the last light behind him, the snow making all things visible. Halfway up Fairy Hill the bus passed him, its windows completely fogged up and the sound of the engine rising to a whine as wheels skidded on the incline.

His feet were cold, but at least he didn't have message bags to carry and his hands could savour the warm depths of his pockets. He winced as he recalled the previous Saturday when he had stood at the top of the hill and cried with the pain in his feet, his fingers frozen around the handles of the bags.

He hated shopping; hated the way most shop assistants tended to ignore a boy with his list while they served all the adults in the shop. He was often left standing while a shop filled and emptied several times, sometimes feeling as if he were going to faint from standing in the one position for so long.

He glanced into Darby's Lane as he passed and saw the falling snowflakes illuminated by the glow from the window of Darby's tiny cottage. Another Christmas card.

There had been nobody on the bus for Ballywaltrim. No footprints crossed the road from Wylie's gate and the snow beneath the bottom light was undisturbed, a dazzling virgin whiteness after the unlit Killarney Road. To avoid spoiling this perfection he skirted around by the garden hedges until he stood under the light with his back to the pole.

He looked up.

An exquisite halo encircled the glowing bulb, snowflakes by the million funnelling into the bright circle out of the blackness beyond, swirling and flurrying in soft confusion before settling with hushed gentleness on the deepening white blanket below. The sound of snowflakes landing is the softest magic in the universe.

He stuck out his bottom lip and blew the snow from his face, then checked his new watch. Four pounds at Delimata's. Took him months to save it up. Nearly midnight.

He started up the Lane, his footsteps crump crumping as they sank in the fresh snow. Some of the cottages were already in darkness. Dad was surprised when he walked in.

'Snow! Yeh look like Daddy Christmas, begod. Haven't looked out all evenin'.'

'Comin' down heavy, too. Lovely out there.'

'I'll make yeh an Oxo. Yeh must be perishin'.'

'Thanks, that'd be grand.'

He got out of his wet things, pulled a chair over to the range and enjoyed the hot drink while his frozen feet thawed out in the oven.

CHAPTER TWENTY-FOUR

The Dargle and Bray Laundry ran a fleet of blue vans which daily traversed much of the counties Dublin and Wicklow. Ray was assigned as helper to John Mooney, driver of 'D' van, whose rounds took in Dun Laoghaire, Dalkey, Killiney and Bray.

At eight thirty on Monday mornings he would begin collecting from houses and flats along Quinsboro' Road, savouring the smell of dozens of frying breakfasts as sleepy-eyed residents opened their doors to his knock. He worked his way along Florence Road and up the long straight Meath Road while his co-helper, Colm Brierton, collected another part of the round.

At designated spots along the way they would leave little mountains of pillowcases stuffed with soiled linen to be picked up by the van-man who was working in yet another area. Later they would join forces and finish the round together. Finishing time was determined by how quickly you could complete your round, and it was a constant race against time as one oul'-lady after another delayed you by not having her stuff ready. There was no going home with the round half done no matter how late it got, and it wasn't unheard-of to be still knocking on doors at half past ten at night.

'What kept yeh?'

'Cattle trouble, missus.'

'What d'yeh mean, cattle trouble?'

'Some a' the oul' cows weren't ready.'

'Isn't that awful, now, they must think yiz have no homes to go to. Step in there a minute, son, while I strip the oul' bed.'

Ah feck.

Back at the laundry the vans were unloaded at what was known as the Hacker's Department, where, it was said, the girls used hammers and chisels to 'hack the shite offa the tails idda shirts.'

In general, customers were conscientious about what they sent to be laundered but there were always those who wouldn't bat an eyelid while presenting you with a stomach-churning bundle that had obviously been on the receiving end of the results of an over-indulgent night at the pub.

Hotels and some of the bigger houses sent their laundry out in large hampers, while at the other end of the scale there were the ladies who only sent their husbands' collars in little round boxes.

In the tourist season the van would be sent on special runs to places like the Royal Hotel in Glendalough or Hunter's at Newrath Bridge. He loved those long drives into parts of Wicklow he had only heard about, and from the first time the van rolled down the hill from Laragh into the lovely valley of the twin lakes he was under the spell of the haunting beauty of that place.

A lady who lived near Bulloch Harbour in Dalkey was a favourite with the boys, who raced each other to her door. She unfailingly answered the doorbell in a long dressing gown that obligingly fell open as she bent down to pick up the milk bottles. However late they might call, those bottles were never taken in before they arrived. She was even known, on the odd occasion, to give an encore, reaching for a receipt or something that would 'fall' from her hand.

'Oops!' she would squeal. 'Naughty me!'

Dalkey was a quaint place with tram-tracks winding through its cobble-stoned main street and a castle on either side of it.

Ray carried a leather bag at his waist, supported by a strap over his shoulder, in which was carried his receipt book and the cash collected. If they got back to the laundry in the evening before the office closed the money was cashed in, but mostly it was brought home overnight, the strap digging into his shoulder with the weight of heavy coins as he picked his way through the darkness of the Dargle Road. At the Silver Bridge he would enter Pembroke Wood and climb the steep paths through the trees by memory. It never occurred to him that somebody might get to know he was carrying cash and decide to waylay him in the wood some night. That sort of thing was rare anyway, but he did have a bit of a scare one time on his way up the wood when he walked full tilt into somebody coming down.

For some reason folk tend to tiptoe when walking in the woods at night; probably so that they will hear the approach of any unseen danger. Unfortunately when two individuals employ this precaution while walking in opposite directions on narrow pathways in the dark, a collision is almost inevitable. Neither party had given more than a surprised grunt when they encountered each other and Ray ran quickly on, climbing out of the wood at the hairpin bend with a thumping heart and crossing the fields by Darley's pond for home.

'Hey, that was me, yeh bollix!' exclaimed Ritchie O'Leary next day at the laundry as Ray related how some fecker had frightened the shite out of him in Pembroke Wood.

He loved to be in the woods on stormy days. The irresistible wildness of it thrilled him to the core; the great trees creaking and groaning, their branches whipped, tossed and tormented by a howling gale. He would run madly down the woodland paths, his own insignificant cries of joy lost in the raging maelstrom, wanting to join in, to be part of this sublime natural chaos.

Once, during a summer storm, he had hidden his clothes under a dry bank and gone running through the wild cathedral that was Pembroke Wood, precious rain streaming down his body. The heavier it teemed the more he revelled in it. He darted and danced; he lay down on the wet leaves of the previous autumn, stood up and let the rain wash him clean. He turned his eyes to the broiling grey of the sky glimpsed through the shrieking boughs, spluttered and laughed out loud as rain-water came down on his face in great drenching splashes from the tree-tops. Black, burn-in-hell mortal sin.

He developed a great love for the mountainy parts of Wicklow, and, having been introduced to many beautiful and interesting places on the van, was soon making his own way around the county by bicycle, which allowed him to explore those hidden glens and valleys not on the van's itinerary.

Solitude before long became precious to him. He would hop on the bike at any opportunity, day or night, and spin off to some remote spot just to savour the tranquillity and the strange magic that seemed to permeate the Wicklow countryside.

He was eternally grateful to his old primary schoolteacher, Seán Donegan, for having introduced him to poetry, and Gray's Elegy in particular, which remained his favourite. Many a night had he fallen asleep reciting it. He could now lean on an old gate and gaze across some sleepy twilit valley where 'drowsy tinklings lull the distant folds' and marvel at how the poet could express such a thing in one short line.

And how many times on dusky evenings in Ballywaltrim had he been on the receiving end of a sharp whack in the face from the big blue-black beetle as he 'wheeled his droning flight'?

He made a point of visiting old country churchyards at close of day, where he would sit in the solemn stillness and converse in his mind with old Tom Gray himself. Someday, he resolved, he would learn to paint and put on canvas beautiful representations of the scenes the Elegy conjured up for him.

He longed to share the wonder he felt with another human being, but there was nobody; nobody who wouldn't think he was a bit gone on top roaming around the wilds of Wicklow by himself where there was divil a thing only mountains, fields and oul' ruins. Well, if they thought he was a freak, so be it, but if the things he saw and felt were things they were unable to appreciate then he could only feel sorry that they were deprived of such joyous experiences.

And the ruins; how could anyone find them uninteresting? Each one, cottage or cathedral, had its own air of mystery to fire the imagination. He could stand before an

235

old fireplace whose hearth hadn't glowed with the warmth of a welcoming blaze for more than a hundred years and ponder what the conversation might have been around that hearth on the night the fire went out forever, or stand on the doorstep and wonder who pulled the door closed behind them for the last time, and under what sad circumstances.

No doubt the laughing voices of children long ago echoed around the same doorstep where now only the lonely wind played, and on winter nights howled in the doorway and out the windows and between the stones of the roofless remains of what had once been the most important place in the world to some long-forgotten family.

But they were not entirely forgotten, not as long as these stones remained and the odd 'freak' happened by now and then seeking ghosts.

At the junction of Vico and Sorrento roads in Dalkey he sat on top of a pile of laundry waiting for the van. It was Saturday and sunny, and he hummed to himself as he looked forward to a long half-day, being near the end of the run and ahead of their usual time for once. A car came down the hill from the Vico Road and as it slowed to turn into Sorrento Terrace he recognized the back seat passenger as the writer Brendan Behan. Pleased to see someone so famous close up, he smiled and waved when Behan looked his way, the smile vanishing abruptly as Behan rewarded him with a moody scowl from the rolled-down window of the car as it passed.

He was mystified at this rude response to his friendly grin. Did all famous people behave like that? He remembered Ma's oft-repeated assertion that Elvis Presley 'wouldn't look at yeh if he came up the lane tomorrow'. Maybe it was true.

The van rumbled down the avenue from the Khyber Pass Hotel and pulled up alongside the little mountain of stuffed pillowcases. Colm jumped out and between them they tossed the lot into the van. Killiney bay sparkled in the midday sun as they sped along the Vico Road, the two lads pillow-fighting in the back while John Mooney warbled 'Stardust' as he drove. At the far end of the curving shoreline Bray Head and the Sugarloaf Mountains beckoned hazily in the heat.

There was one more call and the boys raced each other down the long narrow passageway that connected the road to Killiney beach. They delivered a parcel to Homan's Tea Rooms where live lobsters wriggled in a bucket outside the door.

'Did yiz know', said John Mooney when they scrambled back into the van breathless from their climb up from the beach, 'that it said in the paper yesterday the world is to end at three o'clock today?'

An hour later he was sitting on a rock beneath the Silver Bridge dabbling his burning feet in the shocking cold waters of the Dargle, watching a kingfisher as it darted up and down the river in beautiful streaks of colour, vanishing underneath the bridge and flashing back into the sunlight seconds later.

Refreshed, he started for home, treading through the wild garlic that covered the floor of the wood in the level area that stretched along the riverbank, filling the air with its oniony smell as it was crushed underfoot. Many years ago this space beside the river had been cleared and levelled in a failed attempt at bringing the railway to Enniskerry.

He moved on up the steep path among the trees, his shirt sticking to his back with the exertion. Stopping for a breather, he carved his initials in the bark of a beech and gazed down on the roofs of cars as they took the double turn across the Silver Bridge below him.

Nearing the top of the wood his attention was drawn to a movement at the bottom of a bank down to his right. Peering through the leaves he beheld a couple lying there using their clothes as a blanket and not a screed on either of them. When he managed to drag his eyes to the girl's face he was stunned to recognize the laughing features of Daisy Dunne.

Oh, Holy God Almighty, but she was gorgeous!

He was totally fascinated. The neat, never-a-hair-out-of-place Daisy was lying there with hardly a hair in place, her body gleaming white in the shafts of sunlight. How could she just lie there looking so relaxed and uninhibited? And the things she was doing!

This was different, and the difference was Daisy. In all of those 'lies' the lads had observed the girls had done nothing at all but lie there.

They were all but eating each other now, and Daisy wasn't laughing anymore. He thought the look that had come over her face was somehow familiar. How long did a lad have to be going out with a girl before they did things like that? After all, you couldn't even kiss a girl on the first date. That was a well-known rule. If you broke that one the mot would soon regulate you with a belt in the gob for yourself and would never be seen with you again. It had something to do with respect. Judging by the stage Daisy and her boyfriend had reached they must have been seeing each other for donkey's years.

He prayed nobody would come along the path, heedless of the audacity of invoking the Almighty for such a favour.

Oh, God! They're doing it!

Daisy was bucklepping like a bronco, with the quare lad hanging on like Gilpin for dear life, the beads of sweat glistening on his shoulders. Things began falling together in Ray's brain; those weird animal sounds Daisy was making, he had heard them before. He knew them.

Nurse Blakely!

Holy hand of divine japers...Nurse Blakely!

But that meant...yes, there she goes now, roarin' for Jesus. The very same. It could have been a recording of Nurse Blakely having one of her turns.

Ray was suddenly aware that the scene was fast becoming too much for him. Oh quick, think of something boring.

Twenty-four grains, one pennyweight,

Twenty pennyweights, one ounce... No good...Aw no!

Ah God. Oh feckin' shite. All yukky sticky.

Daisy was laughing wickedly as he turned from the happy scene and moved back down the wood, stumping along stiff-legged like the Frankenstein monster until he found a suitably secluded spot where he dropped the saturated trousers.

Yecch! The only thing available with which to try drying them was his shirt, which was none too dry itself, so he whipped that off as well. The smell was like Parozone.

Hey, the very thing! If Ma got curious he could say he spilled some Parozone on himself, tell her they used it at the laundry.

Mortaler upon mortaler.

Having done the best he could with the spreading stain he laid both garments in a sunny spot to dry off and sat on his moneybag with his back against a tree. He was still shaking.

Nurse Blakely. Nurse flippin' Blakely! All those times. Me worried and she...

Turns how are yeh!

He pummelled his knees with his fists and chuckled to himself. God, it really was a grand old world, if only a lad could join in.

The best part of two hours had passed before the trousers looked respectable enough to walk home in. Daisy and her friend were still in their 'lie' when he tiptoed by the spot again, but looked to be asleep now.

He left the wood and ran down to slake his raging thirst at the fountain. It was twenty past three as he crossed the pond field for home, and no sign of the end of the world.

Ma was at the gate as he climbed through the gap.

'There yeh are, Blades. What kept yeh?'

'Ah, some of the oul' ones weren't ready. Eh, I was just wonderin', Ma, do yeh think I could go back to the hospital in Clontarf to have me other foot done now?'

'What? Is it painin' yeh or somethin'? See, I was right, yeh should've...

'Only coddin', Ma. Only coddin'.'

There was no fear of it. Ever since the operation he only had to stand the wrong way on a pebble or on an uneven piece of ground and his right ankle would turn suddenly, sending red searing bolts of pain to his brain, and each time it happened as he hissed through his teeth in agony he wondered what the hell kind of doctor would butcher a perfectly good foot and call this an improvement.

CHAPTER TWENTY-FIVE

'Poor old Nellie Robbins, Lulu, she's dead, gone the long meander. Found her lyin' in the kitchen, they did. An' wait'll I tell yeh, whatever way she collapsed didn't the teeth fly out of her mouth when she hit the floor an' they found them at the far end of the room. Mustn't that have been a gruesome sight now Lulu? God bless us!'

'For God's sake, Kitty, the things yeh come out with! Who in the name a' Christ wants to hear morbid details like that?'

'They were of good quality, too,' Kitty rambled on regardless of the declaration of disinterest. 'I believe they didn't even break in the...'

'Shut up, for Jaysus sake, will yeh, yeh fuckin' oul' ghoul. Yid turn a body's stomach listenin' to yeh. Have yeh nothin' more pleasant to talk about?'

'Heh-heh, all right, Lulu, I'll say no more if it upsets yeh. I just thought you'd be interested...the poor old soul, Lord rest her.'

'I am interested. I'm sorry to hear about poor Nelly. Just don't keep harpin' on about her shaggin' teeth.'

The dentures of the dead held a strange fascination for Kitty. She collected them. It was one of her less endearing little eccentricities. On the death of an acquaintance of hers she would ask the grieving relatives if she might have the gnashers of the deceased as a keepsake. Just the sort of thing to put to a bereaved individual to bring a little cheer to a sad occasion. Nor did she draw the line at her own family.

When her sister, Aunt Molly, died, she disgusted Uncle Joe with a request for her teeth. Aunt Molly was only in her fifties and was the first of Ma's family to die. Her brother, Jack, was up from Cork for the funeral and came back to Ballywaltrim for tea. Ray had never met him before. Jack was very emotional and made no attempt to conceal his feelings.

'Well, Lulu, this is the first sad break in our family,' he said, 'and I hope and pray it will be a long, long time before the next,' at which point he broke into tears. 'God, Lulu, I love you all. I love every one of you, I do,' and he buried his face in his hands.

Ray thought he sounded like a very caring man, and was sorry he didn't know him better. Ma made no comment on the tearful outburst until Jack and his family had left.

'The sentimental oul' fuck. Did yeh hear him? "I love you all, Lulu." Such tripe! Answer him better to act like a man. So much for the Irish bloody Navy!'

Jack was a Chief Petty Officer stationed at Haulbowline.

The thing that more than any other heralded the end of the 1950s raked the skyline above Messitt's chimney, namely a huge multi-barred aerial at the top of a twenty foot pole, and as that decade drew to a close so too did a whole world. The children of the 'fifties would be the last generation to grow into their teens uninfluenced by the box in the corner.

Ray was steeped. Being Cecil's pal he was invited to watch telly on Sunday nights at number eight, an invitation he took up every week without fail. The reception was abysmal, everything viewed through a chaotic snowstorm, but nobody complained.

Who would quibble about the quality of a miracle?

And besides, when all the lights were switched out and all eyes were fixed on Sunday Night at The London Palladium he could sneak furtive glances at the shapely legs of Cecil's sister, Alice, in the flickering gloom.

Cecil shared his enthusiasm for Rock 'n' Roll and they would get together at Messitt's for noisy record sessions. The newspapers were already carrying headlines like 'Rock 'n' Roll Craze on Way Out - What Next?' but teenagers simply ignored the forecasts of doom and Rock 'n' Roll went on to outlive many of the periodicals that had predicted its demise.

True, there was a bit of a lull after the frenzied excitement of the initial years. Elvis Presley was doing a two-year stint with the US Army in Germany, and Buddy Holly had been killed earlier in the year, but there was a feeling among the kids that the music would survive. Sure wouldn't the King be back next year to get things rolling again?

The last of the old 78rpm records was issued and the new 45s took over, leaving the gramophone truly obsolete. It now stood about six inches shorter than its original height. Ma had taken the saw to it one day in an attempt to even the legs up as it was rocking slightly. Having lopped a small piece from one of the legs she found it was still bocketty, so she had a go at another leg only to find it worse. After several attacks on all four legs she finally decided the thing was reasonably debockettized and the amputee was put standing in the corner on its stumps where it was made to endure the final indignity of becoming a stand for its successor, the new-fangled radiogram.

Old Pat Shortt and his horse-drawn bread-van were no longer to be seen clattering along the roads around Ballywaltrim. They had been replaced by a motor-van that delivered such wonders as ready-sliced pan-loaves, a boon to certain of the Ma's in the cottages who couldn't cut a straight slice of bread to save their lives, and whose kids would appear on the lane tucking into great wedges and doorsteps.

Ray didn't think much of the new pans at all, with their slices as thin as a rasher of wind. It was a good thing they left the batches and turnovers alone.

'Pat's gone, an' the farthin' with him', Ma said, referring to the fact that up until then the weekly bread bill would invariably have farthings on the end.

'That'll be two an' thruppence three-farthin's, Missus, please.'

Now the humble farthing was to be withdrawn from circulation and no longer would the woodcock and the wren sing together in the pockets of the public. No use calling anybody farthin'-face anymore.

Gone too was Dinny Byrne's grocery wagon, and in Bray double-decker buses appeared for the first time, great lumbering monsters venturing outside the confines of their city jungle.

With Cecil and his dog, Ross, he roamed the woods and the slopes of Little Sugarloaf, but now in fields that had once been 'sniving' with rabbits the sighting of one of these timid creatures had become a novelty, so thorough a job had the shameful, man-inflicted Myxomatosis done. On their way from school the children had witnessed the pitiful sight of stricken rabbits, their eyes horribly swollen, sitting in the middle of the road unable to move as the car wheels bore down on them to end their misery.

In Owens's shop he bought a small camera and Mr. Owens loaded it with a free film to start him off. Before he reached home he had used it up, unable to resist clicking it as he walked, wasting it on pictures of the empty road between Bray and Ballywaltrim.

Only occasionally now did he and Val make the long walk from Ballywaltrim to Windgates, but it was still a journey they loved, taking as long as they liked to wend their way along the quiet and, it seemed to them, ever-sunny road to Windgates, climbing roadside banks and walls, and dining as they went on whatever goodies mother nature provided.

Past Lord Meath's Eagle Gates at the entrance to Killruddery and up the gently rising hill to the Half Moon where they were glad to sit and rest awhile with their backs against the high estate walls, Ray on one side of the road, Val on the other. It was pleasantly cool and shady there in hot weather, where the trees that grew behind the walls met overhead to form a green canopy over the sharp curve in the road that gave the place its name.

At night the Half Moon was the darkest, creepiest bit of the road, and when the old neighbours in Windgates told tales of ghostly goings on it was usually 'one dark night an' I batin' for home around be the Half Moon'.

But the Half Moon too was destined to disappear with the 'fifties, replaced by a short bleak stretch of tarmac, no doubt causing much confusion among the old ghosts.

Passing Windgates Well on their left, a little further on they would pause at old Stedman's cottage to admire his laurel hedge, the leaves of which were neatly covered in various shades of 'silver' paper, then a refreshing drink from the pump where the road divides for Templecarrig, one pushing the heavy brass button while the other held his mouth open under the spout, neither caring that the fierce pressure behind the water from that pump invariably meant a thorough drenching from head to toe.

Over the brow of the hill at Upper Windgates, passing the thatched cottages of the ancient village and the entrance to Lily Harris's farm where Ma got the clocking hen whenever she needed some new chicks hatched out. Lily was Mrs. Leeson now but Ma still called her Lily Harris.

Down the steep Windgates hill, racing each other along the middle of the road where more often than not the only thing they might meet in the way of traffic would be Kit Fox's horse-drawn milk cart with its polished brass-bound churns and 'Windgates Dairy' painted on it in gold letters that curved like a rainbow.

Past Fox's gate with its two big stone balls on the piers, and Fisher's with two smaller balls, their excitement growing as they neared their destination. From here they could see the gable of Mrs. McDonnell's cottage, next door to Kitty's. A final short sprint would see them standing on the bottom rung of the iron gate as it swung open against the hedge, crushing the leaves and releasing the scent of laurel that was to the boys synonymous with Windgates. Over the years it had filled their senses as they sported in the front garden, chasing through the gaps in the hedge.

The garden was now a wilderness due to years of neglect, the pigsty and hen-loft inaccessible through the jungle of brambles that had completely taken over the large back garden. The outside toilet too had been overwhelmed and was beyond reach, so the utensil that Kitty referred to as the 'thunder mug' had become their only means of sanitation.

The laurel hedge that stretched down from the gate to within a few feet of the door had grown to a height of twelve feet or more, and a mass of briers extending from the other side of the path joined it overhead leaving only a narrow tunnel to the door. Kitty laughed when they called it the front door; there was no back one. It boasted a brass 52 which they thought a quare thing as there were only ten cottages in the terrace.

A few yards from the door there grew an ancient plum tree, its scraggy head rising above the laurels and lilac. Scratches and grazes were readily offered up as the price paid when the lads raced each other into its branches to get at the few fruits it still managed to produce.

Flecks of mica glinted in the two well-scrubbed granite steps, probably the cleanest part of the house because Kitty, every day after her ablutions, would slosh her basin of soapy water over them and give them a few swipes of the sweeping brush.

'Aunt Lizzie would come back and haunt me if I didn't keep her steps spick an' span. Always down on the knees she was, scrubbin' away like Cinderella.'

From many an old photograph long gone family members stood on those steps and gazed out at their descendants.

The boys chuckled at the way their knock on the sun-blistered door would produce a 'heh-heh' from somewhere inside the house. Kitty liked her forty winks in the afternoon

248

and wasn't averse to a nap at any time if it came to that. The response to their second impatient rap would be a muttered 'Now who the flames...' followed by a shouted 'I'm camming, jost a mowment!'

More muttering and shuffling and the door would shudder open.

'A-haaa! It's the two divil's needles, come to see their Aunt Kathleen. How are yeh, Blades? An' will yeh look at Mister Kilhockeyfax himself!'

Uncle Noel had nicknamed Ray 'Blades'. It had started out as 'Rayser' and then taken the obvious route. Where Mister Kilhockeyfax came from is anybody's guess.

'Come on in. I'm delighted to see yiz. Delighted! Oh, Holy Lord, isn't this a grand surprise! An' yiz're wringin' wet, steamin' like a pair of stewed rabbits. What the divil were yiz up to?'

'The pump at the heada the hill drownded us.'

'That's it, heh-heh, blame the poor oul' pump, yiz little rossies. We'll have a nice cuppa tea anyway.'

Into the dim kitchen cum living room where the fire was poked and the kettle lifted from the hob to sit on it. The rich green of the Wedgewood plates that stood on the shelves of the partition was dulled now by dust, and behind them the boys' beloved trellis room, unoccupied now for more than a decade, had become the household dump.

Shoes off, the cold flags were heaven to burning young feet, while a draught of cool sea air came in through the open window of the tiny pantry where stood the water bucket on a bocketty backless chair. The lads inhaled the familiar fresh 'smell of Windgates' they would joke about in later years, and Kitty sang along with the kettle.

'Can you make a cup of tea, Billy Boy, Billy Boy?

Can you make a cup of tea, charming Billy...delighted, I am!'

And never was delight more genuine.

Then she would attack the loaf with a big knife, holding each slice up to the window to check it for cat hairs, brushing it with her hand before buttering it, while the porcelain figures of the Monk and the Chinaman smiled benignly on the scene from their places on the chiffonier. The unfortunate Chinaman didn't have much to smile about. Having been knocked over and smashed one time, Ma stuck his head back on with Seccotine, but he was left minus his right hand.

Kitty derived great joy from the simplest of things. Once when she acquired a new frying pan she would pick it up every now and then and flick her fingertips against the rim saying:

'Hasn't it got a lovely ding!'

She would discuss the nice tick one of her clocks might have compared to another, and how the one that only worked properly when lying on its face would develop a 'limp' before stopping with a final loud tock of protest if left standing upright.

A rolled-up newspaper was kept near to hand when they sat to eat. It was used to gently whack the cats away from the table, the legs of which had been scratched to shreds by the same moggies.

'Get down, yiz little...whack...Can I not have a minute's...whack...with my guests?'

'Mrkngeiow.'

'Heh-heh-haargh! Honest to Christ, they'd nearly talk back to one like Christians. Down, I say. Down! Little feckers. I might as well be talkin' to the pump. Scram!'

The high dark corners of the room were festooned with 'Irish drapery', as she called the cobwebs, and the pictures on the wall had become so smoke-stained that their subjects were almost indiscernible.

'I must take them down an' give them a lick of a cloth. Haven't seen Grandfather for years, heh-heh. God, he was a lovely man! Eight years in the bed before he finally dropped his knife an' fork, an' never a grumble out of him. Nearly ninety three he was, the poor oul' divil.'

She referred to the picture of old Tom the Horn and his wife taken outside their thatched cottage.

'Is that why they called him Tom the Horn? 'Cause he was a divil?'

'Snoink-snark-caark!' Kitty snorted, choking on her bread. 'Ooh, schluck-schluck, aren't kids a caution. No! Yeh mutt! He used to shout the prices at the fair in Bray, an' they say he had a voice like a foghorn. Now are yeh satisfied?'

'What's a fair?'

'Ah, go an' chew coke.'

On one of the last occasions when the three of them walked down Ennis's Lane to the sea together, Val climbed on top of the Gap Bridge railway arch and she was terrified he would fall.

'Come on down, now, Val. There's a good fella.'

Val grinned at her over the parapet.

'Come down this instant, I say!'

'No!'

'Yeh little demon, yeh. God pardon me today once, will yeh get down outa that before yeh fall down, arse an' pockets, an' break your neck.'

Both of the lads were in stitches now, Kitty's 'God pardon me' always tickled them.

'What'll your Mammy say if yeh kill yourself off there?'

'Shite!'

It was the first time she had heard colourful language from either of the boys.

'What? Oh, goodness, will yeh listen to the little...Come down, you're the divil's flint!'

Encouraged by this reaction, Val decided to push things a little further.

'Feck!' he ventured. 'Get down here at once, bad cess to yeh for a saucebox, or I declare to me paint I'll never bring yeh to the sea again!'

'Oh, feckitty-feckee,' Val sang, grinning and shaking his head from side to side like a sheep in a shower of hailstones.

'Shush for God's sake, you'd make a show of one. Somebody will hear.'

'Fuck!' Val roared at the top of his voice. 'Fuckitty-fuckfuck!'

'Heh-heh, oh Lord, isn't that terrible. I'll warm your wax for yeh when I get my hands...har-hargh-haargh...'

And she went into such a fit of uncontrollable laughter that she fell back on the grassy bank and lay there in convulsions until the lads were beginning to get worried about her. When she finally exhausted herself she lay still for a minute or so to get her breath back, but as soon as she opened her mouth to say something she was off again into another paroxysm.

As they made their way back up the lane folk who shouted greetings over their gates must have wondered what was so hilarious about their comments on the state of the weather. Val wouldn't have dared pull a stunt like that on Ma.

'Wish well and do no harm, that's my motto,' Kitty was fond of saying to the boys. 'Stick to that and you won't go far wrong.'

She claimed she had been a miracle baby, so delicate on arrival in this world that her visit was not expected to be an extended one. She survived, but all through her life maintained that her health remained extremely fragile, and spent an extraordinary amount of time attending doctors of one kind or another. Ma's reading of the situation was that Kitty was an unmitigated hypochondriac, nothing wrong with her a 'good kick in the hole' wouldn't cure, and that she would see them all under the clay.

Which she did.

Val got himself a job in the cellar of the Sunnybank Inn and with three of them working the future began to look a little brighter. Not that they were out of the woods yet, not by a long shot. It just meant that Ma was able to keep slightly less far behind with the bills. Carpet on the floor was still only an extravagant dream, although the concrete of the kitchen floor was now partially covered by a piece of cheap lino. The seats of the kitchen chairs, used for years as sawhorses, were all hacked and gouged so that they resembled the Kerry coastline.

When the annual 'mission' came around Ray attended the grown-ups' retreat for the first time. It involved a week of mass every morning and sermons in the evenings, and the fiery, pulpit-thumping missionary priests put the wind up him with their graphic descriptions of the tortures meted out to those souls guilty of indulging in filthy thoughts and self-abuse. Murder was only in the ha'penny place compared to the gravity accorded this sin of sins in their sermons, and so it was with great trepidation he approached the confessional at the end of the week.

'And do you encourage these thoughts, my son? Deliberately indulge in them?' the priest asked, having listened to the shameful litany.

'Well, eh, not deliberately, Father. They just sort of take over and I can't keep me mind off...'

'Oh, but you must, child, and with God's help you will. Whenever these evil thoughts occur you must think of the suffering of Christ on the cross, and they'll be banished from your mind.'

'Yes, Father.'

'Say five Our Fathers and five Hail Marys for your penance, and pray for me, son. Now say your Act of Contrition.'

'Oh, my God, I am heartily sorry...'

And heartily sorry he was, mainly, it has to be said, because the missioners had made it frighteningly clear that should a lad drop down dead with the sin of impurity on his soul he would burn with the rest of the damned for all eternity, and that meant that after roasting for a thousand million years his punishment would barely have begun. It sounded like a hugely disproportionate revenge for just thinking about something.

Bein' a missioner must be an awful feckin' job, he thought, goin' around makin' God out to be a bollix.

'Watch ye, therefore, for ye know not the day nor the hour' or something like that, they thundered at the quaking sinners.

Terrible words that kept Ray in check for the best part of a week, after which he found himself having to be heartily sorry again.

Ma's religious fervour always increased dramatically following the mission, one of her resolutions being that from then on the family would recite the rosary every evening after tea. They all knelt with elbows resting on chairs around the kitchen while Ma led them through prayers for everyone from Pope to pauper, and especially God's holy missioners who had come here to show us all the way to heaven.'

The 'holy' missioner who molested Val in the sacristy obviously had his own twisted idea of heaven. When missioners or visiting priests arrived they would usually be served by the same altar boy or boys for the duration of their stay. Val never told Ma about the abuse.

Rosary time seldom failed to bring on fits of giggling among the kids, each one endeavouring to make the others laugh, and woe betide the one who proved incapable of controlling his or her tittering valve. The family prayers persisted nightly for a few months, then petered out until the next mission.

CHAPTER TWENTY-SIX

He would do it. No backing off at the last minute this time. He would ask Jane McDonald to go out with him. Jane worked at the Royal Hotel in Glendalough and was always friendly and chatty as he carried the hampers of linen through the hotel. He couldn't understand why she was being so nice but it was lovely and he felt that, inexplicably, it was genuine.

He had come close to asking her several times, but dread of what he considered a highly probable refusal and then having to face her each delivery day afterwards had held him back. Today, as the van hurtled over the humpback bridges of the Roundwood road, he resolved to banish these fears from his mind.

Sure, feck it, she could only say no.

He loved Glendalough, and sometimes cycled the eighteen miles from Ballywaltrim on a fine day to wander among the ancient ruins of the Seven Churches, or follow the Green Road to where Poulanass Waterfall plunged into a pool of purest emerald close to the Upper Lake.

He read every book he could find on the history of the place, and the lovely twin-laked valley became to him the epitome of peace and harmony. St. Kevin had known what he was about when he picked this spot to get away from it all in the sixth century.

Now and again Ray rolled the idea of becoming a hermit around in his head and reckoned there was a lot to be said for a life of solitary contemplation and learning.

But not just yet.

He wondered at the skill of the long-dead monks, creators of the graceful round tower, built to stand guard over the little churches for a thousand years like a great stone Gulliver. Coming down the hill into the village of Laragh the cone of the tower could be seen rising above the treetops, surrounded by the impressive bulks of Derrybawn, Camaderry and Lugduff mountains. That initial glimpse of the glen never failed to stir his heart.

The van swung into the yard at the back of the hotel and when it emerged onto the road again ten minutes later he was in shock.

She said yes. Holy Lamb a' God, she said yes!'

She would be staying with relatives in Dublin the following weekend and he could meet her there. He would have preferred to come to Glendalough, but this being an even greater miracle than the telly he wasn't complaining.

Not on your nanny, Lynch, not on your nanny!

He knew all the rules and stuck to them rigidly. Never attempt to kiss a girl on the first date.

He didn't.

He did, however, go as far as giving her a couple of pats on the back as they parted in Pimlico, which must have thrilled her senseless.

'I'll see yeh at the Divil in Bray next Saturday,' he shouted as he ran off to catch the last 45 at Burgh Quay, wondering what the bemused look on her face was about.

They had gone to the Adelphi Cinema where he had sat like a dummy, rummaging frantically in his head for something to say that wouldn't make him sound like a feckin' loolah, and when he did manage to get something out he was sure it was enough to make a loolah look long-headed.

Maybe he should have tried holding her hand or something. Still, at least she had stayed with him, and agreed to meet him again. Maybe she pitied him, hadn't the heart to tell him to get lost.

Ah, Jaysus.

It was more than likely, he thought, that a good-looking girl like Jane would already have been out on lots of dates, and this concerned him a bit when he pondered how he should go about trying to kiss her on Saturday. Would she be comparing him with other boys and maybe go into hysterics at his clumsiness?

And then there was the greatest worry of all: What if he should become excited and she noticed? Wouldn't any decent self-respecting young-one be off like a cat out a skylight if she found a lad was that way when he kissed her? He hadn't been close enough to her for it to matter on the first date, and as it turned out it wouldn't have been a problem anyway because he was too petrified to be excited.

One thing was certain; he couldn't risk the shame of something like that happening, so he set about devising some means of preventing Jane from noticing.

He experimented for hours. First he tried tying his mickey to his leg, but it kept slipping out. Then he fastened an old belt around his waist and tied a piece of string to it with a loop on the end, which he placed, Pierpoint-fashion, over the head of his mickey.

This seemed a satisfactory solution until he foresaw a potentially serious snag; should he become aroused the string would without a doubt do unthinkable things to his future prospects.

This problem he eventually got around by replacing the loop of string with a small but strong elastic band which would allow for any amorous expansion and yet hold him in place during calmer moments.

Whee! The job's oxo!

On Saturday he donned his homemade harness and set off to meet his first real girlfriend for the second time. It felt awkward and uncomfortable but it would be worth it if it did the trick.

Jane sat waiting at the Divil, her red hair bright in the sunlight, and he found it incredible that this lovely creature was there to meet him. Wasn't there some old saying about meeting a redheaded woman? Was it good or bad luck, now?

Load of oul' diddle-daddle. Willie what-d'yeh-call-him at the Tech was a redhead. Called copper-knob by his cronies, Rusty Bollix by everyone else.

They walked down the Main Street, the tongue in his head once again as much good to him as a woollen hatchet, and went into the Central Cafe beside the church. He ordered fish and chips and approached the jukebox, hoping Jane would mistake his clumsy gait for a swagger. His eyes scanned the list.

'Dream Lover'? Nah! 'Living Doll', 'Only Sixteen', 'Smoke Gets in Your Eyes'... Too soppy. Need somethin' with a bit of go in it.

'One Night' by Elvis. Yeah, that'll send her.

He pushed his tanner into the slot with a do-this-every-day nonchalance, pressed the selector buttons and sat down beside Jane.

'This is a cool number, Jane. Just listen!'

She listened and he again saw that look of amused disbelief on her face as the voice of Mario Lanza filled the little cafe.

'Be my love, for no-one else...'

Aw, shite.

'Hey, that's the wrong one! Honest to God, I didn't even think they'd have such a square record on the jukebox at all!'

Just his lousy luck to push a wrong button at a time like this. No cool self-respecting teenage hip cat would dream of trying to impress his chick with a Mario Lanza record. Only parents and old folk listened to that kind of stuff.

Jane laughed, and then they were both laughing, his bit of a blunder helping to break the ice. As they walked along Herbert Road afterwards he nervously let his fingertips touch hers and suddenly they were holding hands.

Hey-hey, she doesn't mind! She's not pulling away!

He glowed. It was like the sun coming in Sis Cullen's door.

Hope somebody I know comes along so I can show her off. It was a wonder beyond words to him that a girl could like him enough to actually hold hands with him. His heart danced. They sat on a wayside seat at a lonely dip in the road and talked. He was still desperately afraid of saying the wrong thing and there were what seemed to him interminable

261

silences as he chased after some unfoolish comments to make. A dark cloud moved across the sun and a few big drops of rain fell on them.

'It'll only be a sun-shower. Come on, we can shelter over here,' he said, leading her across the road to where an old door was set deeply into a high stone wall. They huddled there as the rain got heavier and she was so close he couldn't help putting his arms around her. She immediately reciprocated by wrapping hers around him.

Her face was so close, so lovely.

And oh God, her lips...

She didn't slap his face or turn away when he let his lips brush, then press, hers. It was the softest, lovingest, most wonderful thing he had ever done. He held another warm, living human being in his arms.

More wonderful still, she held him.

He felt her arms tighten about him and knew inexpressible joy. She felt so slight he was fearful of hurting her. She inspired in him a gentleness he had never known existed, but now recognized as part of loving and something he would gladly carry with him to anyone he might be lucky enough to get close to for the rest of his life.

Every fear and doubt seemed to melt away in this his first real embrace, and he did not want that summer shower ever to end as it pattered about them. He felt like crying.

He buried his face in her hair and longed to let the tears flow freely; tears of gratitude, joy and relief at what felt like finding a home after a long weary search he didn't even know he had been on.

He was straining at his harness, but if Jane noticed anything she said nothing.

It would be all right.

He would have to marry her, of course. This had to be some kind of miraculous fluke, and if Jane really liked him she must be blessed, or cursed, with a rare and quare class of taste. If he should lose her there would surely never be another girl who would look at him twice.

The sun came back out, turning the road into a dazzling mirror and the last few raindrops to bright dancing diamonds. Water dripped from the seat so they left the doorway and walked on, now with their arms about each other, until it was time to turn back for Jane's bus, which would leave the Town Hall for Glendalough at half past six.

They joined a group of people sitting around the base of the Divil.

'Is it really supposed to be the Divil?' Jane enquired.

'Not at all! It's somethin' to do with Lord Meath's coat of arms. A wyvern they call it, whatever the hell that is, but the Bray folk have always called it the Divil, so me Dad says.'

'It's an awful lookin' yoke.'

'Yeah. He had the Town Hall built too, yeh know.'

'Who did?'

'Lord Meath. Gave it as a sort of gift to the people of Bray, an' the Divil with it…here's the bus!'

They climbed aboard the quaint old St. Kevin's bus. It was packed with laden Saturday shoppers returning to their homes along the high road to Glendalough, and in the narrow aisle they stood crushed together, a not entirely unpleasant circumstance.

The smells, familiar to Ray, of fowl foodstuffs like pollard and Layer's Mash, filled the bus, and it was abuzz with chattering voices. Passengers bore bags and parcels piled high on their laps, and more bags and boxes were stacked at the front of the bus. On the racks overhead day-old chicks cheep-cheeped in perforated cardboard cartons, and a couple of framed pictures of Glendalough hung behind the driver's partition and swung to and fro with the motion of the vehicle.

As they pulled in at the end of the lane he gave Jane's hand a last squeeze before jumping off, having arranged to meet her in Glendalough the following weekend.

What a day! What a glorious unbelievable day!

Strolling around Bray like Lord Muck, holding hands with a smasher like Jane McDonald.

And she had kissed him, black tooth and all!

There was no understanding it; the age of miracles was truly not yet past.

His feet hardly touched the ground as he skipped up the lane.

'Hello there, Mrs. Dawson! Grand day, thank God.'

'Powerful weather altogether son,' the old lady looked up from closing her gate. 'Begod, an' you're in quare good form, grinnin' like you're after winnin' the Fifty.'

Fifty! More like fifty million.

He stood and looked around him before opening his gate.

Catty Gollagher, Killiney Hill, Bray Head, Little Sugarloaf. The woods, the fields. Everything wonderful.

Should he mention Jane at home? How the blazes could he resist talking about her when he wanted to shout it to the world? But he was not in the least confident that Ma would share his new-found delight in life. After all, she only had to see a couple kissing in a film or in a magazine photograph and she would want to know why they always had to bring 'that sort of rubbish into everything', so God only knew how the idea of her own son going out with a girl might strike her.

He would sing dumb.

CHAPTER TWENTY-SEVEN

1977

The hedgerow opposite number fifteen was bright with dog roses for the last time; the bulldozers would soon arrive to rip the roots from the earth, and the growth of centuries would be obliterated in an hour. From where he stood on the dusty bank at the gap he could hear their mechanical clanking as they worked on the new housing estates that had already reached out as far as Darby's Lane, a mere two fields away.

A patchwork blanket of rooftops covered Fairy Hill, and a church of ultra-modern design stood at Boghall corner in place of the vanished Little Wood. The cottages looked small and vulnerable as they waited to be engulfed by the unstoppable wave of two-storied 'progress'.

Many of the older folk had passed away and the voices of the few remaining would never be enough to make a difference.

'If that hedge goes it'll be the end of Ballywaltrim,' they would say among themselves as they helplessly watched the approaching threat to the peaceful way of life in the Lane.

And Butler's field, now spreading its green carpet under the warm sky of the last summer of its existence, would soon be only a memory buried beneath countless tons of concrete and tarmac. A caressing breeze sent silver whispering waves fanning down the meadow towards Massey Cottage; a softly breathed farewell.

The ratchety call of the corncrake would never again float across the lane scraping the stillness of a summer's day.

Summer would come again to Ballywaltrim, but the stillness was gone forever.

Darley's pond was no more, filled in and built over. Nowhere now for the little mother water hen and her chicks to swim, or for the gangly heron to feed. Unthinkable now for kids to attempt riding down Fairy Hill on an old wardrobe door fixed to the wheels of a pram as he and Val had done many a time in the days when the intervals between cars allowed for such thrills.

No more playing roadside marbles all the way home from school during the marble season, or stopping to chat with Mister Hopkins, the Council road-man, as he boiled his billycan for tea on his roadside fire. Did anybody even know when the marble season was anymore?

The very stars themselves were dimmed as the serried ranks of streetlights marched out from the town to rob Ballywaltrim of the night.

The woods were forsaken as playgrounds, most of the once well-trodden paths so completely overgrown that it was difficult to believe they had ever existed. The Tarzan vines in Pembroke wood had been destroyed during tree-felling in the 1960s, and while the fabulous slides in Hodson's had survived so far, they were unknown to, or at any rate ignored by the new generation of children who sat at home in front of their boxes and demanded to be entertained.

A great freedom had been lost; the freedom of children to roam the countryside, and to be gone all day with no need for parents to give it a second thought.

The great beeches overlooking the slides still bore the stretched and misshapen initials of the children of the 1950s whose laughter rang among the trees and seemed to echo down through the years in the happy gurgling of the Hollybrook stream.

The simple act of walking, once a normal essential everyday part of living, had been replaced by the motor car, and old Shanks' mare was only resorted to in emergencies.

Journeys were once undertaken on foot that would now be looked upon with incredulity. In those days the sound of your footsteps counted. It was all that was heard as you walked the roads, apart from the songs of birds and the scurryings of small wildlife in the hedgerows.

In a mixed group the steady rhythm of the footfalls blended hypnotically as the miles slipped by, the heavy clumping of the men playing bass in the orchestra to the dainty tapping of the ladies' heels, the scuffing of the adolescents and the pattering of the little ones. Not much in the way of conversation. All minds concentrated on the journey and anticipating the cries of surprise and delight from the relatives or friends being visited.

Soon it would be considered essential to give notice of an intended visit so that houses might be put in order, delight and surprise falling victim to pride and correctness.

On reaching the top of a hill a soft 'Thanks bitta God' might be heard from the adults, then onwards, pressing ahead steadily, unaware that they were part of a world on the verge of extinction, passing quietly into the realm of the gone.

Ray left the gap and walked slowly down the lane, turning his steps in the direction of Little Sugarloaf, a good place to be when the rocks are warm and the mountain paths dusty.

He went up through lush green doomed fields, and from his favourite viewing rock he gazed over the valley and wondered how it could all look so peaceful and normal, as if nothing had happened, yet felt at the same time reassured that this was so.

His eyes found and rested upon the tiny white cottage that was home. Far down there Ma was laid out on her bed in the front room. In the back room, standing against the wall still rolled up, was a grand bit of carpet.

Printed in the United States
By Bookmasters